Scrap Wood
WHITTLING

19 Miniature Animal Projects with Character

Steve Tomashek

Fox Chapel
PUBLISHING

Dedication

I'd like to dedicate this book to my farm family: my wife Randi, our daughter Winona, our son Wyatt in the stars, plus the countless critters who inhabit our land. I feel charmed to live among them, enjoying their warmth and strength.

Acknowledgements

I want to acknowledge my best friend, mentor, and all around cool guy, the late Glenn Gordon. His wit and wisdom are dearly missed. Glenn was a skilled woodworker, writer, and photographer. I worked with him photographing my carvings periodically over the course of almost ten years and enjoyed his friendship through biking and chats over coffee. His knowledge and vision helped me to see the forest through the trees.

I want to acknowledge my sister, Ann Johnston. Her support gave me the space to develop my skills as an artist when it was not clear that I could make it work. Without her help I couldn't have survived as an artist and this book never would have been written.

I also would like to acknowledge the tool makers, Del Stubbs and Peter Lucas among them, for their craft and artistry in making the instruments we whittlers use.

© 2022 by Steve Tomashek and Fox Chapel Publishing Company, Inc., 903 Square Street, Mount Joy, PA 17552.

Scrap Wood Whittling is an original work, first published in 2022 by Fox Chapel Publishing Company, Inc. The patterns contained herein are copyrighted by the author. Readers may make copies of these patterns for personal use. The patterns themselves, however, are not to be duplicated for resale or distribution under any circumstances. Any such copying is a violation of copyright law.

All step-by-step, getting started, and technique/tool photos by the author. All glamor photography by Mike Mihalo. The following images are credited to Shutterstock.com and their respective creators: p. 6 (ancient horse): Villy Yovcheva.

ISBN 978-1-4971-0168-5

Library of Congress Control Number: 2021941284

To learn more about the other great books from Fox Chapel Publishing, or to find a retailer near you, call toll-free 800-457-9112 or visit us at *www.FoxChapelPublishing.com*.

We are always looking for talented authors. To submit an idea, please send a brief inquiry to acquisitions@foxchapelpublishing.com.

Printed in the United States of America
First printing

Introduction

The state of Minnesota, where I grew up and spent most of my adult life, is known for an abundance of soft, clear basswood and long, cold winters, which are excellent conditions for an aspiring woodcarver. A blizzard is the perfect time to stay inside, grab a chunk of wood, and whittle away the hours; such was my childhood. From my bedroom window I could see two giant basswood trees on the boulevard; the city erased them when they started to hollow, but they each could have fueled lifetimes of whittling. It may not have been destiny, but I was pointed toward carving and ran with it.

My niche has always been animal miniatures. I've chosen not to work at a consistent scale but rather to carve in sizes that relate to the human hand. I've created a menagerie, a collection of exotic animals. Some took ten minutes to make; some took ten hours. My miniature menagerie has thousands of carvings and hundreds of species representing years of exploring the animal world. I've studied and created animal art for over twenty years, and this book allows me to share some of that experience.

The object of this book is to set forth a collection of miniature animal projects that meet learners at all levels of experience and that require only a knife. Fundamentals and simple projects are explained in depth to start the beginner on the path to realize the fun and fulfillment of whittling. The novice can slowly gain confidence and skill as they learn to carve intricate details using illustrated step-by-step instructions. More experienced carvers will find value in the projects that focus on the major themes in my process and art form. Every learner will benefit from the multitude of tips, ideas, and plans as they explore this unique style of painted sculpture.

I organized this book by skill level; basic information and techniques are explained and illustrated in the first chapter, and then a group of simple step-by-step projects and plans are provided for the beginner. The next set of projects introduces increased complexity and detail work with a group of jumping animal figures. In the next set, each project examines a different theme while providing step-by-step instructions for whittling a diverse cast of miniature animals. The last set of projects includes dioramas that explore concepts like scale and space while thinking and creating inside a box. Interspersed throughout are tips and tricks gained through years of experience.

Please enjoy exploring this miniature world of animal wonder!

—Steve

Table of Contents

98

26

32

92

A Brief History of Carving

The current, standard definition of whittling is the art of using a knife to sculpt objects out of wood. It's a form of woodcarving, but without chisels, gouges, mallets, chainsaws, or angle grinders. If woodcarving is poetry, whittling is haiku: the constraint of the form is also what makes it unique and elegant. It's deceptively simple; knife meets wood. The beauty of a single tool means there's just one tool to master. It's a populist and portable art form: for the cost of a knife, wood, and a few accessories, you're ready to take your workshop with you.

Humans have been carving for a baffling number of years. Before written language, before farming, even before dogs, we were whittlers. Some of the earliest miniature sculptures have been found in caves in Germany: miniature ivory animals, 30–50,000 years old. They mark the emergence of the completed human species, a craftsperson. Working ivory with stone tools was not a five-minute project; these figures signal the

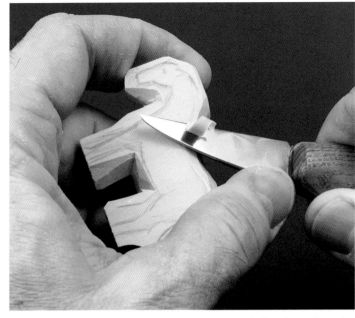

The horse was one of the first animals to be recorded sculpturally in the human record.

dedication of a community to the craft. Humans had been tool tinkerers for 2 million years already; wood of all dimensions would have been the primary material. The presence of these miniatures raises many unanswerable questions; but what we know for sure is that these humans had the luxury of sitting around whittling.

In the United States, whittling became popular after the Civil War with the growth of transient populations. It was a perfect pastime for the itinerant laborer, and many became anonymous masters of a repertoire of items that included wooden chains, ball-in-a-cage, animals, and religious figures. The advent of the Boy Scouts helped spur further interest, so much so that whittling was long considered the preserve of boys and old men. Nowadays, anyone can try their hand at the peace and peril of sculpting wood with a knife.

The thought of whittling may seem obsolete in an era running at the speed of the newest technology. The distraction our electronic gadgets provide us is intoxicating; the slow work of whittling is, for some, the antidote. The creative place we can inhabit while whittling is absorbing, meditative, and challenging. The end product is a tangible object, unlike the many ethereal tasks we perform via computer. We can hold our creation, the work of our hands; it connects us to the real world and reaffirms that we humans are forever artists and craftspeople.

This ancient ivory carving, discovered in the Vogelherd cave in Germany, dates back to at least 29000 BCE and is one of the earliest known carvings of a horse.

Getting Started

Wood

Of the 60,000 species of tree on our planet, a handful produce woods that are easy to carve. Wood is highly variable, even within the same species. Wood that is dry or "seasoned" will be harder to work than freshly cut or "green" wood, but green wood has a tendency to split if it's not dried properly. Carving wood must be taken slowly: hands will get sore, knives will dull, and it can be a frustrating and dangerous first experience if the wood is not suitable. Common woods like maple, birch, walnut, and oak are not recommended for beginners. You may find good carving wood at hobby stores, lumber mills, or via mail order; knowledgeable tree trimming services and fellow woodworkers are also possible options.

Recommended

Basswood (*Tilia americana*), a hardwood, is the best wood for beginners and has been used for some of the most accomplished woodcarvings ever made. Trees of the genus *Tilia*, which includes basswood, linden, and lime, produce wood that is famous for its uniform texture, and it's one of the lightest woods formed by deciduous trees. Usually free of knots or irregularities, it carves easily and holds detail well. The wood is plentiful and inexpensive. Whittling it requires little strength, and your knives should stay sharp a long time. Forest-grown basswood that has been air dried for at least 6–12 months will be softer than kiln-dried basswood. Wood harvested from near the Canadian border will work easier than wood from southern sources. It's some of the best carving wood in the world.

Basswood

Softwoods

Coniferous trees produce softwoods that are usually easy to whittle, but there are exceptions and caveats. Knots, resin, and splintering are the biggest problems with many softwoods. You must take extra care if you need to carve details. Trees grown in colder climates or at higher altitude will provide denser, more fine-grained wood due to a slower rate of growth.

Scots pine (*Pinus sylvester*) is widely cultivated for construction lumber, but as a result it's wildly variable in quality. Look for pieces with no knots and a tight grain. While it's easy to work, details will present a challenge and require extra caution. Wood should be seasoned for 6–12 months before using. High resin content may also interfere with finishes.

Norway spruce (*Picea abies*) is also used for construction, but it is perhaps best known as the common Christmas tree. Like pine, it should be seasoned for 6–12 months before using. It will be easy to whittle as long as there are no knots present, but take special care when working in small dimensions.

Scots pine

Norway spruce

Yellow cedar (*Cupressus nootkatensis*) grows along the northwest coast of North America; quality wood outside this range may be expensive. It is easy to carve and has a fine, straight grain. It holds detail better than most softwoods due to its slow growing conditions. Yellow pine, white pine, and Douglas fir are also reported to carve similarly well if grown under the right conditions.

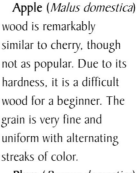

Yellow cedar

Hardwoods

If, like me, you have access to a fruit orchard, yearly pruning will provide a bounty of branches especially suitable for miniature projects. Fruit tree wood is generally rather hard and not recommended for the beginner, but the typically reddish brown colors take on beautiful natural finishes. Consider using the woods for simple projects like keychains or pedestals for your carvings.

Pear (*Pyrus communis*) wood has a very fine, straight, and uniform grain and a smooth and consistent texture. It is one of the finest hardwoods in Europe, but it is rare and expensive outside Europe. It's an excellent whittling wood that holds detail well, but expect to sharpen your knife often and only remove small pieces of wood with each knife stroke.

Pear

Cherry (*Prunus serotonin*) wood is popular and expensive due to its attractive color and gentle figure. That figure can also make it more difficult to whittle than its hardness would predict.

Cherry

Apple (*Malus domestica*) wood is remarkably similar to cherry, though not as popular. Due to its hardness, it is a difficult wood for a beginner. The grain is very fine and uniform with alternating streaks of color.

Apple

Plum (*Prunus domestica*) wood is often knotty and irregular but has a fine, tight grain. It's easier to work than most fruit woods, and it can usually be found in just small amounts. It's the most colorful of the woods listed here, often containing streaks of red, pink, and purple.

Of the harder woods, I use boxwood (*Buxus sempervirens*) for its ability to hold detail. The grain is fine, straight, and uniform, and the wood is hard and strong. This wood is often used for netsuke miniatures, a Japanese form of ornamental figure carving. When I've used it, I employ files for details and saws or a Dremel to rough out the figure.

Plum

Boxwood

Tools

To carve the projects in this book, you'll need to assemble a small collection of tools. You'll need at least one whittling knife with blade protection, sharpening tools, safety equipment, a first aid kit, a miniature pin vise and drill bits, a saw, a set of acrylic paints and brushes, a pencil, a pen, a drawing book, and sandpaper. When I travel with my mobile workshop, I pack these items in a cigar box (sans saw) and with a little pile of scrap wood. I hit the beach or find a stump in the woods to sit on and let the chips fall where they may.

Knife: The most important tool in the whittler's toolbox is the knife. It must have a carbon steel blade that is hard enough to hold an edge but not too brittle. The shape and size of the handle and blade are personal preferences. I prefer having one

large-bladed knife and one smaller detail knife. The knives I used for this book are the 2" (5cm) Harley knife made by Pinewood Forge and a few detail knives from OCC Tools, David Lyon, and Peter Lucas. For an inexpensive all-purpose alternative, I recommend the Kirschen 3358 carving knife with a Murphy style blade. When it's not in use, keep your knife sheathed for your own safety and for preservation of the cutting edge. If your knife did not come with protection, build your own blade sheath from leather, cork, or rubber tubing.

Sharpening tools: To keep your knife razor-sharp, you'll need a strop and stropping compound; to repair a damaged blade, you'll need sharpening stones. Strops are pieces of either smooth or suede leather; sometimes one or both versions are

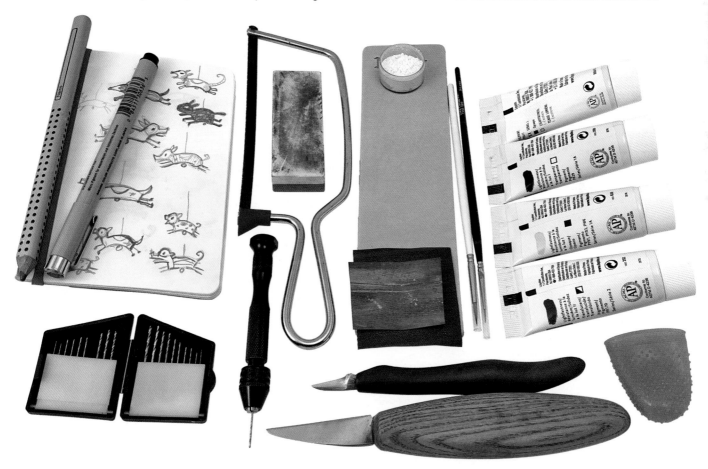

From left to right: pencil, pen, drawing book, micro drill bit set, coping saw, miniature pin vise, sharpening stone, carving knife (Pinewood Forge), detail carving knife (Peter Lucas), sandpaper, leather strop, aluminum oxide stropping compound, paintbrushes, acrylic paints, rubber finger protector

fixed to opposite sides of a piece of wood. Stropping compound is an abrasive powder or paste; examples include green chromium oxide and white or gray aluminum oxide. Sharpening stones come in sets of varying coarseness: Arkansas, ceramic, diamond, and India stones are all adequate. At a minimum, you'll need one coarse and one fine stone—for example, a 600-grit and a 1200-grit.

Safety equipment: I recommend that beginners start with a safety glove to use on the hand holding the piece of wood; the gloves resist slicing cuts, but not stabs. Some whittlers, including myself, use leather, rubber, or taped fingers that function like an extra layer of skin. Though they will not stop forceful cuts, they will absorb low-intensity cuts. I wear a rubber finger to keep the knife off my carving hand thumb. If you're sanding wood, wear a mask to keep harmful dust out of your lungs. Keep bandages handy; while it takes some effort to pass a knife through wood, skin offers little resistance. A poke with a knife will ache, but a long slicing cut will require stitches or worse, so be safe.

Miniature pin vise: A pin vise is a miniature drill clamp attached to a handle that you turn by hand. You use it to drill small, precise holes. This allows you to control the depth, location, and direction of a hole to a high degree of accuracy. These can be purchased together with a set of drill bits that fit the chuck of the tool. In this book, you will use the pin vise to drill mounting holes in your carvings so that you can insert a toothpick to hold the carvings while you paint them.

Saws: You'll need to cut wood to the right dimensions at the start of each project. Multiple types of saws come in handy to cut up lumber and rough out pieces of all different dimensions. Handsaws like a coping saw should be used on wood that is secured by a clamp. A scroll saw will work if the wood you've got is already cut into small pieces. A bandsaw is the best all-around tool for cutting and roughing out. I also use a miniature table saw to make the small boxes in the last set of projects.

Paint and brushes: Use a quality set of acrylic paints to color your projects. You'll need at minimum five colors of paint: blue, yellow, red, black, and white. For brushes, a couple of #1 and larger round brushes of moderate quality and a high-quality liner detail brush will do the trick. The detail brushes used in salons to paint fingernails work well.

Other tools: Round out your toolbox with a pencil for drawing on wood, a pad of paper and pen to record your ideas, and sandpaper (150-, 300-, and 600-grit) for smoothing surfaces, if desired.

Sharpening and Tool Maintenance

Keeping your knife razor sharp is an important skill to learn, as it not only makes whittling easier and more enjoyable but also safer: a dull knife is dangerous because it requires more force to cut, thereby sacrificing control. Avoid damaging your knife unnecessarily; use it only for wood and avoid metal, especially other knives. Protect the blade during storage and do not use it like a pry. Before the blade dulls and whittling becomes more difficult, strop the blade to fine tune the cutting edge, about every 20 carving minutes, depending on the hardness of the wood. If stropping doesn't sharpen a dull blade, sharpen on a stone to repair or rebuild the cutting edge.

The Kirschen Schitzmesser (carving knife) comes new with a rough factory ground Murphy blade that must be sharpened on a stone before it is used on wood. Some knives come pre-sharpened, but eventually you'll need to sharpen the blade yourself.

Stropping

Stropping is all that should be needed to keep a blade razor sharp for a very long time. Some carvers use leather strops without compound, but adding an abrasive speeds the process. Stropping compound is often used with suede leather but it can also be applied to smooth leather. Rub the abrasive into the entire surface of the strop. Repeat applications every fifth use; when the compound gets thick and crusty, remove it with heat and a butter knife. To strop a knife, lay it flat and apply firm pressure as you pull it backward across the strop. Keep the bevel of the blade flat through the entire motion. The cutting edge should slightly compress the leather, allowing the abrasive compound to sharpen the microscopic bevel at the edge. A trail of black residue should be left on the strop, indicating that metal is being removed. With coarse stropping compound, a few strokes on both sides will bring a dull blade back to razor sharp.

To prepare a leather strop with aluminum oxide powder, spread the powder evenly on the entire surface of the strop with the applicator.

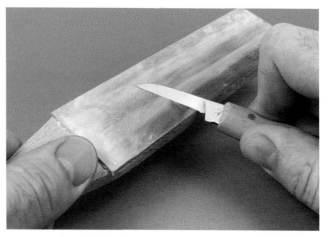

Strop your knife by firmly pressing it flat and pulling it backward several times on each side across the leather.

Honing

When a blade has a bad factory finish, is nicked, or stropping fails, it's time to hone. First, secure a 600-grit stone to a stable surface. Apply water to the stone's surface and bring the blade to it. Using your hands on both the handle and the blade, lift the unsharp side of the blade about 1/32" (0.8mm) and stroke the knife on the stone backward on both sides until a tiny burr appears along the entire edge. Remove this burr by honing on a finer 1200-grit stone or on a leather strop; a bare piece of smooth leather works well for this.

There are as many opinions and preferences for sharpening as there are fish in the sea, so I have several recommendations to help the beginner master this skill. First, buy an extra knife on which to practice sharpening daily and find what works for you. Second, find a fellow woodcarver with experience to show you in person. Third, watch instructional videos of whittling knives being sharpened. Not everyone learns best by written instruction, and this is one skill you need to become an expert at. In the end, you will save countless hours, prevent injuries, and make your knives last a long time.

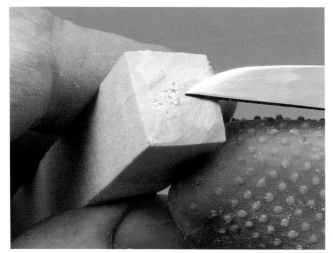

If your knife tears the end grain of a piece of basswood as shown, it is very dull or damaged and requires sharpening on a stone.

A two-sided stone, like this one from Kirschen, provides a coarse and fine option. Here the knife is being sharpened on the fine ceramic side. The back of the blade is raised slightly and is ready to be pulled backward across the stone.

Designing Your Project

This is of course a project book, but it will also teach you how to branch out and create your own projects and patterns. With that in mind, let's examine a good design process.

When you decide to make a new, specific object or animal, research it before you grab a knife. This may include finding photos of the subject as well as what other artists have drawn, painted, or sculpted. In the case of animal subjects, videos will show how its body changes as it moves and reveal details that are often hidden in still photographs. Directly observe and interact with the animal if possible (and safe). Kernels of ideas may come from poems and fables, figures of speech, or mythology. From Egyptian hieroglyphics to Gary Larson's "Far Side" to the poem "Panther" by Rainer Maria Rilke, my own inspiration for a design has come from a diversity of sources.

A good way to stretch possibility within your repertoire is to temporarily adopt a foolish notion while designing a figure or to use whatever failure occurs while carving. I once ruined the head of a cat while carving, lopped it off, and carved a replacement head for it to hold in its paws: a zombie cat. Not everything is a home run: I have a box of broken and abandoned carvings and a stack of drawing books full of ideas that I will never execute, but they do live on in my creative space as a valuable resource.

When I design, I make quick sketches to record each idea. Often, plans are ground out, mashed together, and polished over the course of a session. Keep what works; set aside what doesn't and move on. I doodle freely and randomly, often working on multiple subjects until I have maintained a flow of drawings that leaves me options. Select a plan and roughly transfer it to wood. Continue to draw and mark the wood as needed to help guide where or where not to cut.

If you're having difficulty visualizing how to proceed with sculpting in three dimensions, you're not alone. As a novice, this problem vexed me so deeply I dreamt about it. One effective method to help train your brain is to build a clay, wax, or wire model of the figure or piece you're trying to whittle. A carving school in the Obergammerau, Bavaria, requires this of their students before they are allowed to even touch a piece of wood.

Often, my own thoughts are the source of my ideas, but sometimes a chance conversation or suggestion hands me a commission or the answer to a question I hadn't thought to ask. The inspiration that comes from meeting someone whose heart beats in time with yours is a gift the Greeks called a muse. The spark of creativity can come from many places, as long as you are humble and open to where it leads you. It could be the final piece of something that's been puzzling you, or the first step on an entirely new path.

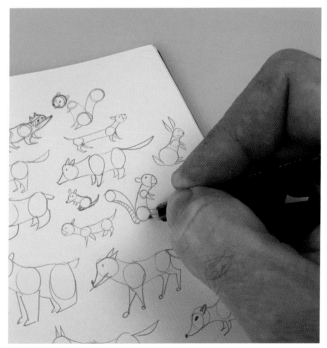

Assembling a drawing with circles and shapes is an effective, simple method.

Repeating the same idea multiple times will help prompt you to draw it differently each time. In the case of this fox study, some follow a familiar pattern, but others veer off from normal considerably.

These drawings of kiwis and snipes explore the movement and cartoonish nature of the animals.

Carving Techniques

Wood is strong in the direction of the grain and weak perpendicularly; keep this in mind as you transfer a design to wood and while you whittle. Long legs, tails, ears, or horns need to be positioned to take advantage of this strength as much as possible. Where this is not possible, consider whittling them separately and pegging them into place. As you work, you'll notice that it is easier to cut with the grain rather than across it. Grain will also dictate how you go about whittling details: one uncontrolled or poorly planned stroke of the knife is all it takes to lose a figure's foot, nose, or ear.

Keeping your fingers safe is paramount and requires maintaining good technique and control. Always keep your knife sharp and never whittle when you are tired, angry, impatient, or impaired, or there will be blood. Maintaining control of the knife means only removing small bits of wood with each knife stroke; as you apply more force, you have less control over what happens next. Because whittling is a subtractive sculpting technique, meaning material is removed to reveal the figure, err on the side of removing too little rather than too much. Use repeated cuts at the same location to achieve a larger result. Whittling is not a race. Your hands will gain strength, control, and micro motor skills only over many hours of practice time. Until then, take it easy on your fingers.

Basic Cuts

The most basic knife stroke is the **paring cut**. The paring cut is performed like one pares vegetables or peels a potato: flex your knife hand while cutting toward yourself in a controlled manner in order to shave off a piece of wood. It is the easiest method, but it is also potentially dangerous, since you are cutting toward your thumb; for that reason, it is not recommended for beginners. If you choose to employ this method, protect your thumb from micro cuts with a layer of leather, tape, or rubber.

A **push cut** can accomplish much the same thing as a paring cut with less potential for injury. The "push" is often carried out by the thumb of the hand that is holding the wood. Apply pressure to the blunt side of the blade or to the thumb of the knife hand. Also apply some pressure with your knife hand and guide the blade away from the body. You can also perform a push cut without help from the thumb—it's just there to boost the amount of force applied.

Combination cuts require multiple knife strokes that come together to remove material. With the **V-cut** and the **stop**

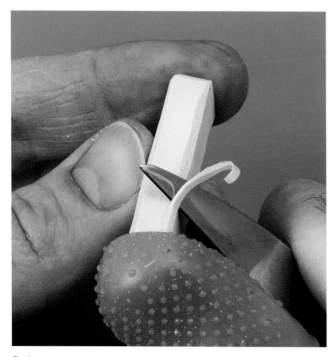

Paring cut

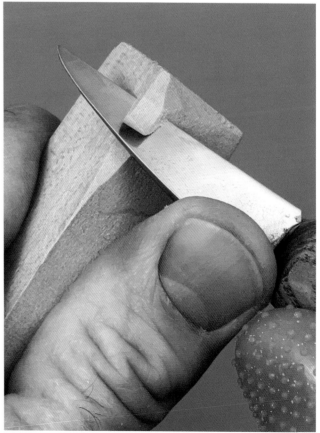

Push cut

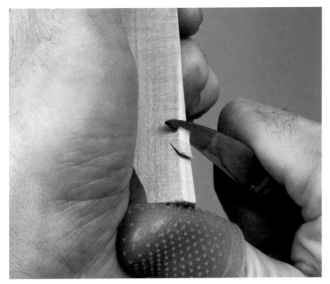

V-cut (two-stroke cut)

Stop cut (two-stroke cut)

In general woodcarving, the term "**stop cut**" is typically used to denote a single cut into wood that does not remove any wood itself, which is then met by another cut that does remove wood. In this book, the term "stop cut" is defined as a two-stroke cut with the first stroke perpendicular or 90 degrees to the wood surface and the second stroke angled to meet it, similar to a V-cut.

cut, establish a boundary with the first knife stroke and use the second stroke to chip out the piece of wood in front of the first cut. For the V-cut, each stroke is at an angle to meet in the middle. For the stop cut, the first stroke is perpendicular or 90 degrees to the wood surface and the second stroke is angled to meet it. Three or more cuts in combination can make **tent-shaped** and **triangle-shaped** notches: make two knife tip incisions connected like a V under the surface, and make a third cut to chip out the wood.

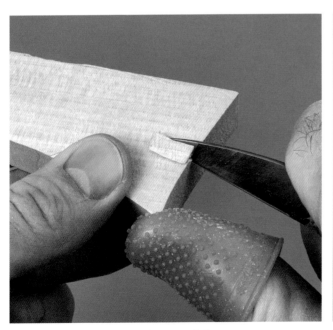

Three-stroke combination: tent-shaped chip

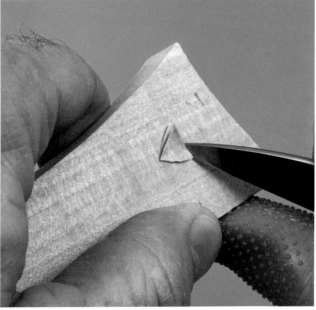

Three-stroke combination: triangle-shaped chip

Painting and Finishing

There are many ways to finish wood, but for the purposes of this book, we will focus on my preferred method: painting with acrylic paints. I don't prime the wood and I don't use varnish, as it tends to attract more dust and dirt than paint alone. If a figure painted with acrylics needs cleaning at some point in its lifetime, use a tissue dipped in alcohol or soapy water. See some alternatives to acrylic paint at the end of this section.

I recommend buying a basic set of four or five quality acrylic paints and mixing your own colors rather than using dull, cheap colors straight from the bottle. For this book, I use a set of five Liquitex paints, including Ultramarine Blue, Cadmium Yellow Medium, Naphthol Crimson, Mars Black, and Titanium White. You can make an infinite number of colors by mixing these five. Some colors will dry darker than they appear when wet. Test colors and combinations on your palette before applying to your carving.

Even for the consistently small projects in this book, you will need more than just one small paintbrush. Brushes don't just come in different sizes, but in different shapes, like flat, filbert, round, spotter, and liner, which are good at achieving different things. If you are on a budget, I recommend a range of round brushes, because it is the most versatile shape, and a liner detail brush, which can also do the job of a spotter brush. Use larger brushes to apply base coats and large color fields. Use smaller brushes to make eyes, dots, spots, hash marks, details, and outlines. Be sure to wash paint thoroughly from your brush every few minutes as you are painting so that the paint doesn't dry in the bristles and ruin the brush.

I recommend high quality acrylics to paint your carvings. Colors should be brilliant and colorfast.

I approach painting as with design: I start with a blank canvas, albeit curved. I look to fabric patterns, paintings, illustrations, toys, and the skins of nature itself to find inspiration. Oftentimes I choose playful schemes with naturalistic or fanciful palettes. I try to grow my knowledge by studying masters of color like the Russian painter Wassily Kandinsky, who wrote a whole book on the topic.

Using an old CD as a palette, create a color wheel to learn how colors mix and explore the relationships between colors. Try out color combinations. See what colors look good together.

Paintbrushes (from left to right): Filbert, #7 round, #1 round, #2 liner, #18/0 liner. Different sizes and shapes serve different purposes.

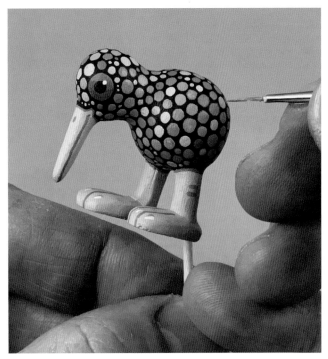

This snipe has not been painted with realistic colors—don't feel restrained by reality!

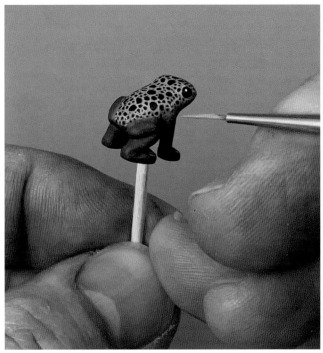

Mounting your work on a toothpick will allow you greater control while painting.

Some subject matter demands a certain blueprint (skunks, for instance); for others, like dragons or dinosaurs, the door for the imagination is wide open, a blank canvas.

The nature of miniature plays an oversized role in determining the balance of color, pattern, and complexity in a painted skin; a thumb-sized figure requires special treatment. First, mount it on a toothpick: drill a small hole in an inconspicuous spot and either glue or simply wedge the toothpick into place. In most cases, the hole can be left after the carving is complete. Holding the carving with a toothpick makes it easy to observe and will keep your fingers from smudging the paint. Make a precise painting plan and start painting large areas of color first, getting progressively more detailed. Painting at this scale is meticulous and painstaking; it requires a peaceful workplace. For the smallest elements, you may want to hold your breath and feel your heartbeat as you paint—I do this.

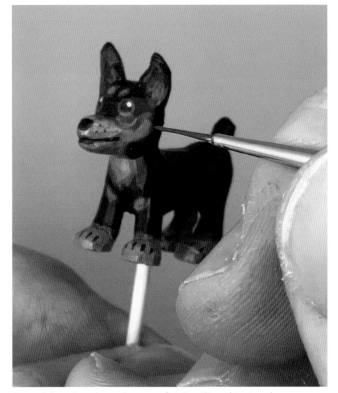

A small liner brush works great for detailing this tiny dog.

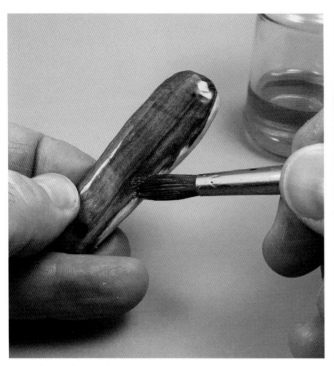

Using boiled linseed oil brings out the natural colors of wood, like this plum keychain.

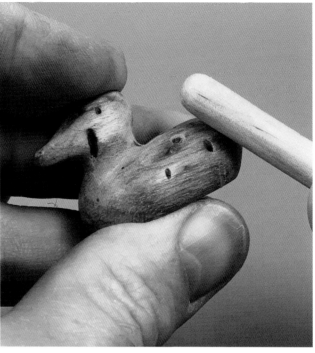

Use wood to burnish wood (butternut, in this case) for a shiny and classic finish.

Alternative Finishing Methods

Some effective alternatives to painting include using stains, polyurethane varnishes, or, for a more natural wood finish, boiled linseed oil. Burnishing, which is rubbing the wood to produce a shiny surface, is a cost-free option, while pyrography, the burning of designs in wood with specialized equipment, is an art form in its own right employed by many woodcarvers to adorn their work.

For any project in this book, you can decide whether to recreate the real animal's markings or get creative with something fanciful!

Projects

Easy Projects for the Beginner

Pages 20–43

If you have never picked up a knife before, I recommend that before you begin these projects, you first whittle sharp points on sticks and carve a cube into a ball to get a general idea of the capabilities of the knife and the resistance of the wood. Carving a ball will also teach you about wood grain and how important it is to stay aware of the direction of the grain as you whittle. I've planned these projects for ease of carving. The plans for the figures were designed with the wood grain in mind so that details are less prone to snap off. If you do break off a feature, you can either glue it back on, paint it on, or invent a whole new species of animal.

Intermediate Projects for the Apprentice

Pages 44–73

Germans love to make new words by combining ones that already exist. "Springtier" or leaping animal is an unusually succinct example, and apt, since these projects are the carving equivalent of a quick sketch. The creatures are meant to be made in quantity, for it is by practice and repetition that one gains proficiency. The point of an apprenticeship is to gain experience: to train the muscles of your hands to coordinate with the thoughts in your head. Keep it simple and aim for precision, not perfection. The focus for these projects is on the details of the head and ears.

Themed Workshops

Pages 74–109

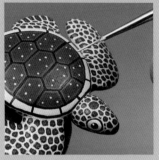

In the traditions of the trades that date back to medieval times, the person who has completed a period of apprenticeship becomes a journeyman, traveling away from their teacher to work as a day laborer for a period of time. In that spirit, these projects are designed to give you some things to think about on your carving journey. It is by reflecting on what we do that we can find fulfillment in the simplest of tasks. By making things with a keen intention, we realize a tangible reward, an object imbued with the thoughts behind the process.

Working inside a Box

Pages 110–133

Building a miniature world, a microcosm, is a feat of intense perspective—though bounded by a nutshell, we are free to make a kingdom of infinite space. Working within a literal container is a powerful tool for play. For these projects, we employ visual tricks and a sliding scale, tinker with perception of depth, and disrupt the idea of distance. Working inside a box doesn't mean we sacrifice creativity and innovation. It merely sets a simple limit—the maximum size of the carving—and makes no other demand.

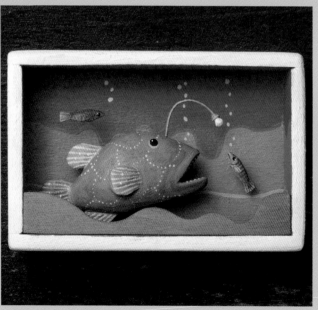

Mouse

We've got a mouse plague in our region. The fields are full of holes, and the pitter-patter of paws every night calls for extreme measures. If ancient Egyptians made miniature animal amulets to protect against the forces of nature, it's worth a try. Abstract artists entertain the idea that there is power in pure forms; it is in that spirit that I designed the head and body of this mouse as a teardrop shape and the appendages shrunken. It all looks deceptively simple, but the precision can be tricky. Beginners should be ready to improvise. For instance, tails are fragile; in a pinch, a strip of leather can be substituted for wood.

Materials & Tools

- Wood: ⁷⁄₁₆" x ⁷⁄₁₆" x 2" (1.1 x 1.1 x 5cm), grain running in the longest dimension
- 1 toothpick
- Carving knife
- Hand protection
- Pin vise with ¹⁄₁₆" (1.6mm) drill bit
- Paintbrushes: #1 or larger round paintbrush, #10/0 liner or smaller detail brush
- Paints: red, blue, yellow, white, and black to mix shades of purple, pink, and light blue

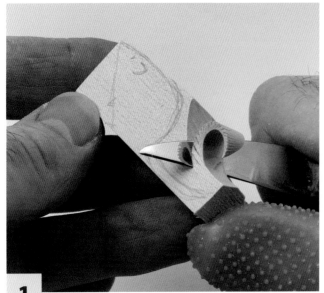

1   **Rough out.** Transfer the pattern to the wood. Using paring and push cuts, rough out the opposite corners of the block under the chin and above the tail. Leave enough material on the belly for the paws.

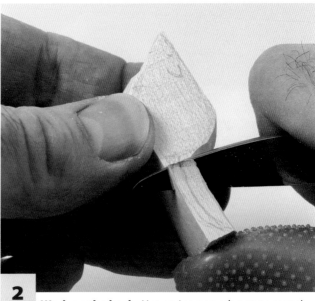

2   **Work on the back.** Use paring or push cuts to round the edges of the back. Narrow the tail to about ¼" (6.4mm) so that it is not too fragile, then make stop cuts with the first knife stroke to establish the boundary of the back.

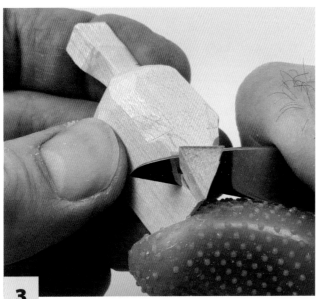

3   **Shape the head.** Bring the head of the mouse to a point. Make a small groove with a stop cut to mark the back of the ear, then use paring or push cuts to narrow the head of the mouse and bring the cuts together at the nose to form a point. Round all of the edges of the head and nose with paring cuts. Make long strokes so that the surface remains smooth, not choppy.

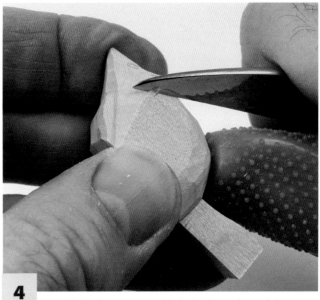

4   **Establish the ears.** Establish the boundary of the ear with the first cuts at a 90-degree angle. Cleanly match the first cuts with secondary knife strokes that start from the mouse's back. Use paring cuts to blend the front of the ear with the face. Use paring cuts to smooth the area behind the ears with the rest of the body.

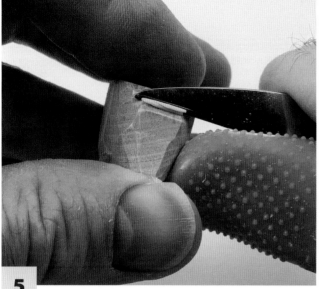

5 **Work on the paws.** Establish the front and back paws with paring and push cuts. Mark the boundary of the belly on the side of the figure and make sure not to cross it. Carve toward the nose. Make push cuts in front of the front paws and paring cuts between the front and back paws, building a separation between the two sets.

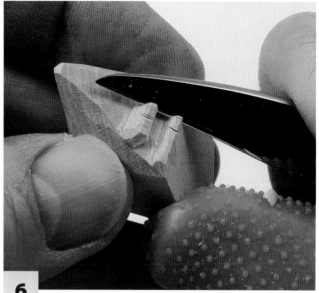

6 **Separate the left from right paws.** Start with V-cuts to separate the paws, then use stop cuts to expand the gap and establish the boundaries of each paw. The second strokes of each stop cut should be flush with the boundary of the belly. Be careful not to cut too deep: stay aware of the line marking the boundary of the belly.

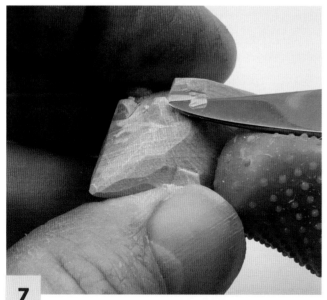

7 **Separate the back paws and the body.** Use stop cuts; make a shallow first knife stroke on the top and side of the paws and follow that with a stroke directed toward the first cut from the side of the body to chip out the material. If you apply too much force, the paws will be lost, so take it slow.

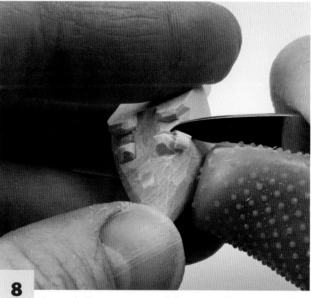

8 **Smooth the area around the paws.** Use paring and push cuts to clean up the area between and around the paws so that the belly is smooth and flat, using just the knife tip and being careful not to nick the paws. Look at the figure from multiple angles to make sure the body is symmetrical.

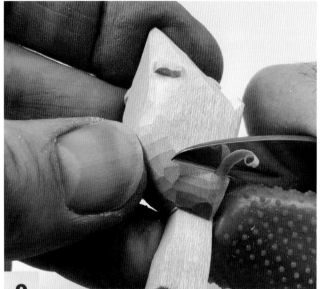

9 **Round the edges on the bottom of the figure.** Using paring or push cuts, start near the rear paws and extend to the tail. Make several long knife strokes to remove the material so the edges are smooth and the knife mark facets are curled around the edge. Blend the cuts with the sides of the body. Then clean up the curves on the entire body, especially where the body meets protruding features.

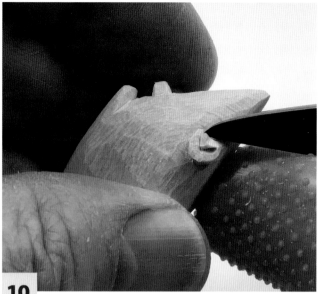

10 **Carve the insides of the ears.** Use a three-stroke combination cut to establish this. First make two incisions with the knife tip following the curve of the ear's edge. Start about ⅓₂" (0.8mm) from the tip of the ear and continue to keep this border, making a shallow incision that runs all the way around each edge to the base of the ear. With the third knife stroke, this time at the base of the ear, chip out the material.

11 **Carve the tail.** Draw a curved guideline on the tail wood, then narrow the tail with a series of paring, push, and stop cuts. Use stop cuts at the base of the tail and paring and push cuts to narrow the rest of the tail. Take off material equally over the entire tail and pay attention to the grain of the wood to determine whether to push or pare. As the tail gets thinner, remove smaller amounts of wood. Finally, drill a ¹⁄₁₆" (1.6mm) hole in the bottom of the figure and insert a toothpick to hold while painting.

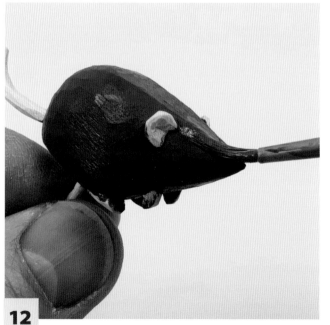

12 **Start painting.** Mix blue, red, and white paint to create a purple color for the body. Apply several coats, spreading the paint evenly until the wood is thoroughly covered. If you notice loose bits of wood in the crevices between the paws and belly, use the tip of the knife to cut them off before you proceed.

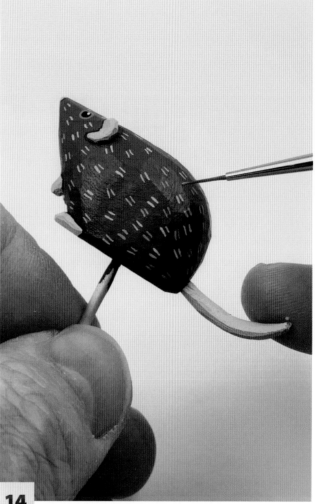

13 **Paint details.** Mix red, white, and a touch of yellow to create a flesh tone for the ears, nose, paws, and tail. Apply two coats. Mark the location of the eyes and mouth with a pencil and paint them in with black paint. Mix a lighter and darker version of the purple base color by adding white and black to two separate portions of the original mixture. Outline the borders of the pink features with a darker purple and the black features with the lighter purple.

14 **Paint features and patterns.** Mix three shades of light blue from white and blue paint. Make random double hash marks of each of the three colors over the entire purple area. Mix a new flesh tone, making it slightly darker than the first by mixing in a little light blue. Apply this color to paint hairs on the tail and inside the ears, toes on the feet, and nostrils on the nose. Finally, paint white reflection dots in the eyes.

Pattern

Penguin Family

Penguins are as far from a typical bird as Antarctica is from my backyard feeder. Best known for sporting tuxedos and an almost mechanical tottering, they could be mistaken for a lost colony of plutocrats, only more charming. From the artist's perspective, penguins can be carved in a variety of dynamic poses despite their stilted stride: they swim with elegance underwater, and their terrestrial form is easily caricatured. For this project, I've designed a form in which the beak follows the grain of the wood so it's less likely to snap off accidentally as you carve. I've also included a pattern for a baby penguin so you can carve a whole family.

Materials & Tools

- Wood for each adult penguin: 7/8" x 7/8" x 2 7/8" (2.2 x 2.2 x 7.3cm), grain running in the longest dimension
- Wood for each baby penguin: 3/4" x 3/4" x 2" (1.9 x 1.9 x 5.1cm), grain running in the longest dimension
- Several toothpicks
- Carving knife

- Hand protection
- Pin vise with 1/16" (1.6mm) drill bit
- Sandpaper: 200–400 grit and 600–800 grit
- Paintbrushes: #1 or larger round paintbrush, #10/0 liner or smaller detail brush
- Paints: red, blue, yellow, white, and black to mix shades of orange, gray, and light blue

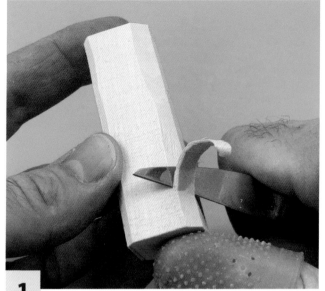

1 **Rough out.** Transfer the pattern to the wood. Use paring or push cuts to round the edges on the long corners. Don't carve too deep—leave extra material outside the pattern lines for future removal. Redraw marks that have been lost due to carving, especially those marking where the head and beak start.

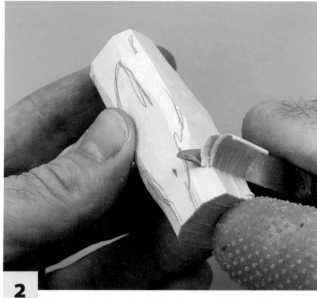

2 **Narrow the head and beak area.** Using paring or push cuts, remove more material from the head and beak area, leaving extra material for future removal. Carve on all sides of the head and beak, taking off equal amounts on every side.

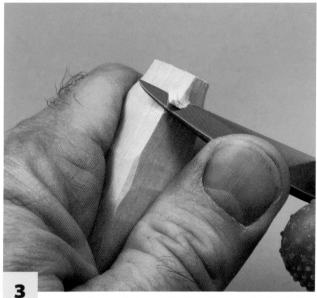

3 **Narrow the beak from all sides.** Redraw the beak if necessary. Using push and paring cuts, remove more material from the area of the beak. Take off more material from the sides and less from the top and bottom of the beak. Leave extra material for future refinement. Blend the head with the beak transition using paring cuts.

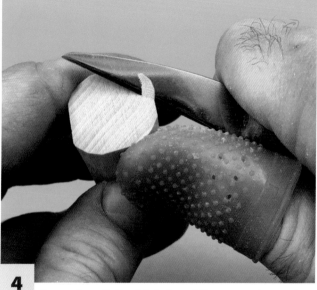

4 **Carve the tail.** Establish the tail first use paring strokes to shave off the edge on the bottom rear of the figure, then using a V-cut to make the dip between the tail and the back of the penguin. Start the first knife stroke at the tip of the tail and cut toward the head. Match this cut with one in the opposite direction starting approximately ½" (1.3cm) from the tip of the tail. Blend the cuts for the dip with the back and clean up any mismatched cuts.

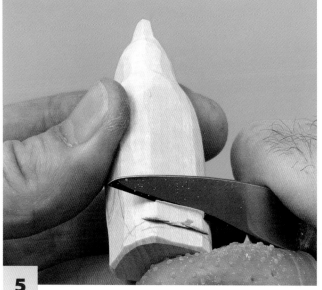

5

Establish the feet. Using a V-cut, start with a knife stroke approximately ⅛" (3.2mm) above the bottom of the figure and meet this cut with a knife stroke from the belly. Continue to excavate this groove with similar cuts, making sure not to cut too deep from the direction of the belly so as not to break off the feet. Use paring cuts to blend the groove with the belly and smooth the curves of the feet.

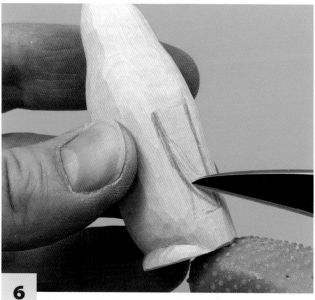

6

Establish the boundary of the wings. Redraw the wings if necessary; make sure they are symmetrical. Using the tip of the knife to a depth of about ⅟₁₆" (1.6mm), make incisions along the entire boundary of each wing. Direct the angle of the knife nearly perpendicular to the surface of the figure.

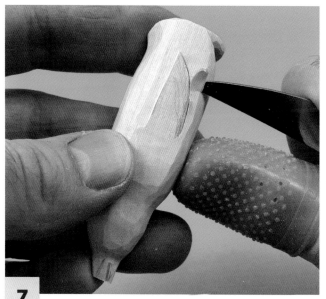

7

Relieve the wings. Using the tip of the knife, carve away the wood in front of and behind each wing. As you cut, keep the tip of the knife at the incised cut mark without penetrating the boundary of the wing. Blend what you've excavated with the curves of the body using paring or push cuts.

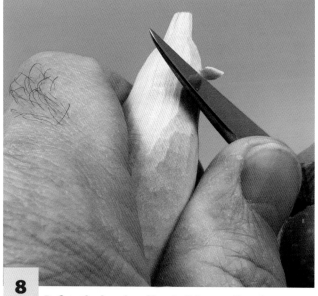

8

Refine the head and beak. Using small push or paring cuts, blend the head with the body. Pay special attention to the curves at the front and back of the head as it transitions to the body. Using the pattern, measure the dimensions of the beak and pay attention to symmetry as you narrow the head and beak to their final sizes. Establish the transition between the head and beak with stop cuts. Carve the outside curves of the upper and lower beak.

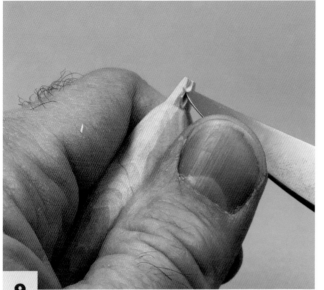

9 **Redraw and carve the gap in the beak.** Using the tip of the knife, make incisions on both sides between the upper and lower beak halves. Expand the V-shaped groove with controlled push cuts, being careful not to put too much force in the knife strokes. Once the gap is established, make push cuts using the tip of the knife to further expand the gap until you reach the drawn boundary line.

10 **Sand.** Start with a coarse (200–400-grit) sandpaper to smooth the wood, rolling the sandpaper to create a curved sanding surface. Avoid the beak; focus on the curves of the body and head. Then switch to a finer (600–800-grit) sandpaper. Sand the same areas over to get a smoother finish. Sand the beak, but be careful to not remove too much material. Finally, drill a ⅟₁₆" (1.6mm) hole in the bottom of the figure and insert a toothpick to hold while painting.

11 **Paint the black areas.** Draw the outlines of the color fields on the wood. Thin some black paint with water to make it easy to apply, but not so thin as to cause the grain of the wood to raise. Apply two coats of black paint to the area on the back, wings, feet, and head. Use a detail brush for increased accuracy near the borders. Leave an unpainted border around the eyes.

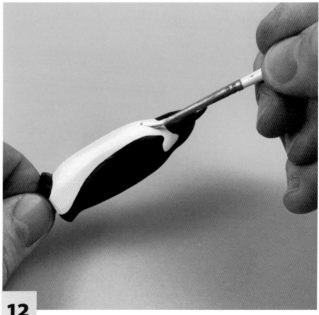

12 **Paint the white areas.** Apply white paint to the belly and cheeks of the penguin. Use a detail brush as you paint closer to the borders. Apply two coats of white to all but the cheeks of the penguin, as these parts will need a coat of light orange later.

13 **Add oranges.** Mix yellow, white, and a little red and blue paint to create a light orange color. Mix the light orange color with white to create two additional progressively lighter orange colors so that the lightest orange is nearly a cream color. Apply the darkest of the light orange colors to the topmost part of the penguin's cheeks. While the paint is still wet, use each of the lighter oranges to blend with the previously painted orange area to achieve a gradation from orange to white from the top of the cheek to the belly. Mix red, yellow, and a touch of white to create a new orange color to paint a small, thin crescent on the lower bill.

14 **Add details.** Mix black and white to create three gradations of gray. Outline the eyes with the lightest gray, paint the toes with the medium gray, and paint dots on the wings and body with the darkest gray. Mix the light gray mixture with blue to create a steel gray blue color. Outline the border between the black and white/orange areas with this new color.

Patterns

Duck

A male duck on our farm was "courting" a lady duck when he slipped off her back and landed on his. He lay there, paddling the air with his feet, until I rescued him. I love ducks because they look absurd on a regular basis, whether they're marching in line, dabbling in mud, or watching the sky for hawks. It's tempting to think they're just being jesters performing slapstick, drawing our attention to life's comedy. The legs and feet that are the focus of most of the physical humor and clumsiness can also be the weak points of a woodcarving. Due to the singular direction of wood grain and the perpendicular nature of legs and feet, carving them as one unit would mean one or the other is precariously weak. For the beginner's sake, this project focuses on the fluid, sculptural quality of the head and body while simplifying the wobbly undercarriage by using toothpicks and a base.

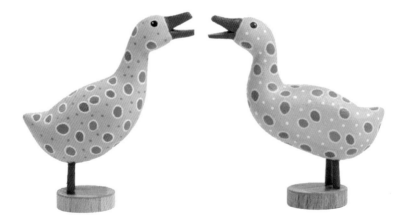

Materials & Tools

- Wood: ½" x 1" x 2" (1.3 x 2.5 x 5.1cm), grain running in the longest dimension
- Several toothpicks
- Dowel or twig: ⅝" (1.6cm) dia. or larger, piece cut to ³⁄₁₆" (4.8mm) long/thick
- Carving knife
- Hand protection
- Pin vise with ¹⁄₁₆" (1.6mm) drill bit
- Wood glue
- Sandpaper: 200–400 grit and 600–800 grit
- Paintbrushes: #1 or larger round paintbrush, #10/0 liner or smaller detail brush
- Paints: red, blue, yellow, white, and black to mix shades of yellow, orange, pink, and green

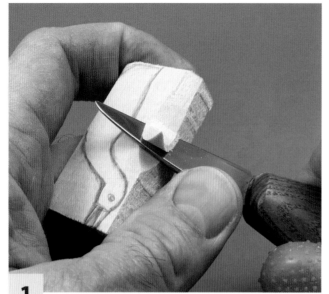

1 **Rough out.** Transfer the pattern to the wood. Rough out the area above the back and below the head. Use paring or push cuts to remove the material, carving close to the marks you've made to show the boundaries of the duck. Establish the curves of the top and bottom of the head and neck.

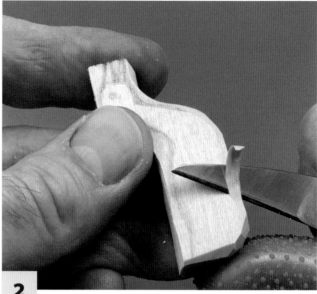

2 **Round the edges of the body and tail.** Using paring or push cuts and cutting almost across the grain, carve the tail section to a round shape until it blends with the sides and bottom of the body. Also use paring or push cuts to round the edges between the sides and top of the body.

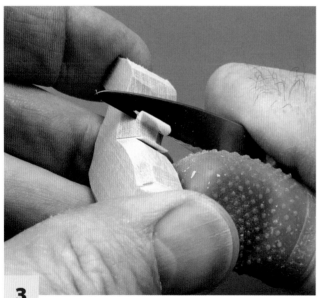

3 **Begin to refine the body.** Narrow the tip of the tail with paring or push cuts and blend it with the body. Use shallow V-cuts to establish the dip in front of the tip of the tail. Start the first knife stroke close to the tip, cutting toward the head, then meet that cut with a knife stroke starting in the middle of the back, slicing in the direction of the tail. Use a shallow V-cut to establish the dip behind the neck and blend the dip to the neck and back with paring cuts.

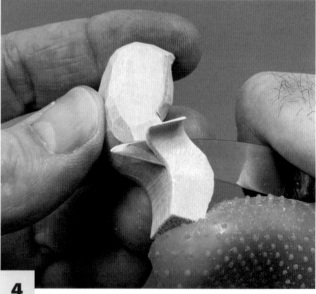

4 **Narrow the neck, head, and bill.** Use paring cuts to reduce the thickness of the head and neck to approximately ¼" (6.4mm). Use paring or push cuts to make the bill area thinner still, about ⅛" (3.2mm) wide. Be careful not to remove too much material; make sure that you leave the head and bill symmetrical.

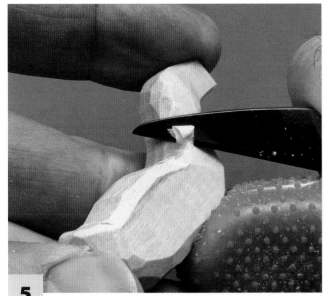

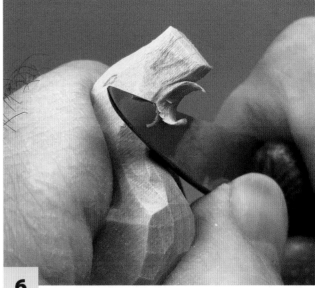

5 **Narrow and blend the neck.** Using paring or push cuts, reduce the thickness of the neck symmetrically. Pay attention to the direction of the grain. Knife strokes on the back of the neck should start at the back of the head and slice in the direction of the body, while knife strokes on the front of the neck should proceed from the body toward the head. Blend the neck with the head and body using paring cuts to soften the edges.

6 **Carve the bill.** Redraw the duck bill on the wood. Use paring cuts to establish the top of the bill and remove the tiny bit of extra material from in front of the lower bill. Use V-cuts to define the bottom of the bill at the point where it meets the head; use paring cuts to blend this transition area with the head. Use paring cuts to finish establishing the bottom of the bill all the way to the tip.

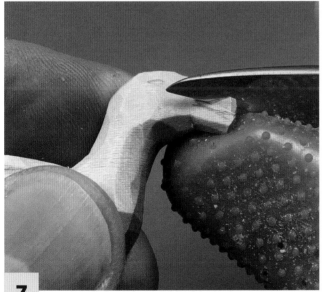

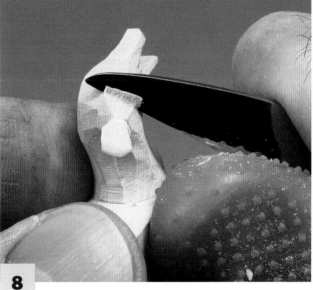

7 **Carve the gap in the bill.** Start with a V-cut on both sides of the bill, being extra gentle and precise so as not to overshoot or break the bill. With the tip of the knife blade, use paring cuts following the boundary of the V-cuts to connect the notches you made on each side. Once the gap is a singular V-shaped notch, use paring cuts with the tip of the blade to further expand the notch all the way to the drawn boundary marking the inside of the bill.

8 **Shape the head.** Narrow the top half of the head so that the area around and behind the eyes is narrower than the cheeks. Use paring or push cuts to remove material from the top half of the sides of the head. Use paring or push cuts to blend and smooth any sharp edges on the head and establish the boundary between the sides and top of the head and the bill. Observe the area in great detail and from every angle; correct any symmetry problems with paring cuts.

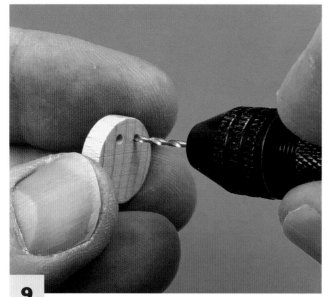

9 **Make the base.** From a twig or dowel that is at least ⅝" (1.6cm) in diameter, cut a ³⁄₁₆" (4.8mm) piece. Mark and drill two ¹⁄₁₆" (1.6mm) holes near one edge approximately ¼" (6.4mm) apart. Drill two ¹⁄₁₆" (1.6mm) holes in the bottom of the duck body the same distance apart. Drill these holes so that the legs are approximately perpendicular to the bottom of the duck's bill.

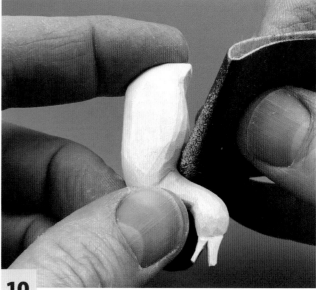

10 **Sand.** Start with a coarse (200–400-grit) sandpaper. Where there is too much material to just sand off, use paring cuts to bring the area into alignment. Avoid sanding the bill with coarse sandpaper. Once you're satisfied with the general shape of the carving, switch to a finer (600–800-grit) sandpaper. Use the finer sandpaper to fine tune the shape of the bill and smooth the figure overall.

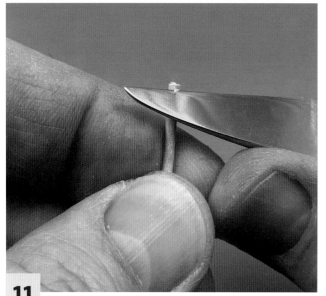

11 **Create the legs.** Make two ½" (1.3cm)–long cylinders from toothpicks by scoring the circumference of a toothpick under a sharp knife blade and snapping at the cut. Shave each end to ¹⁄₁₆" (1.6mm) in diameter, starting each taper ³⁄₃₂" (2.4mm) from the end. Apply wood glue to each end and insert the ends into the holes to attach the duck to the base. Finally, drill a ¹⁄₁₆" (1.6mm) hole in the bottom of the figure and insert a toothpick to hold while painting.

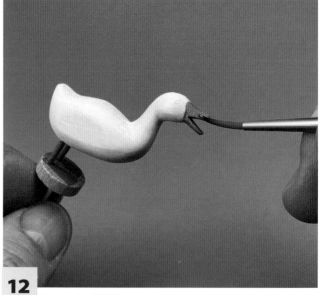

12 **Paint the bill, legs, and base.** Mix red and yellow and a touch of white paint to create an orange color to paint the legs, feet, and bill with two coats. Add a touch of blue into the mixture to create a brown color and paint short hash marks for the toes and nostrils. Mix yellow and a little blue paint to create a green color and apply two coats to the base of the figure, between the feet.

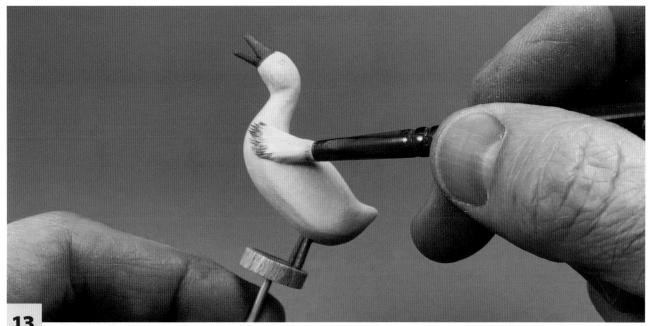

13 **Paint the main body.** Mix yellow with a little white paint to create a lighter yellow color. Apply two thick coats to the figure's head and body. Leave a thin border along the legs and bill unpainted for now, then paint it in more accurately with a detail brush. Mark the eye location with a pencil and paint the eyes using black paint. Mix the yellow with more white to create an even lighter yellow color to outline the eyes. Add a white spot in each eye.

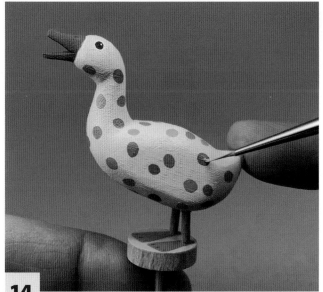

Pattern

14 **Add details.** Mix blue and white paint to make a light blue color; mix red, yellow, and white to make a peachy pink color; and mix yellow, blue, and white to make a light green color. With these three colors, make a random pattern of egg-shaped dots on the yellow body of the figure. Mix yellow and white paint to make a light yellow color and outline the dots with this color.

Dinosaur

Dinosaurs disappeared from earth millions of years ago, but in our modern age they've taken up residence again, this time in toy boxes and fed by the imaginations of children. For artists wanting to delve into the world of the Jurassic, those plastic toy versions are inexpensive study models representing a huge diversity of subject matter. For this project, I designed a Brontosaurus, the "thunder lizard." Its rollercoaster curves have a natural artistry and present a wonderfully round canvas for painting. Since the direction of the grain of the wood will mean that the legs will be weak, I've designed them shorter and thicker than is natural to give the beginner a better chance to carve them without breaking. The painting requires a lot of precision brushwork to pull off, but even a close approximation will look good.

Materials & Tools

- Wood: ⅞" x ⁹⁄₁₆" x 3½" (2.2 x 1.4 x 8.9cm), grain running in the longest dimension
- 1 toothpick
- Carving knife
- Hand protection
- Pin vise with ¹⁄₁₆" (1.6mm) drill bit

- Sandpaper: 200–400 grit and 600–800 grit
- Paintbrushes: #1 or larger round paintbrush, #10/0 liner or smaller detail brush
- Paints: red, blue, yellow, white, and black to mix shades of green and pink

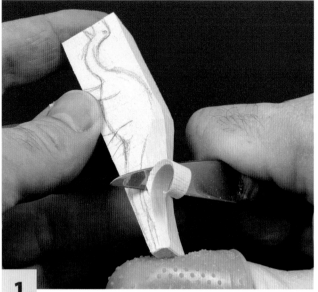

1 **Rough out.** Transfer the pattern to the wood. Carve out the material above the tail and below the head and neck, using paring or push cuts. Don't carve all the way to the lines on the pattern, but rather leave a little extra wood for strength as you work on the rest of the figure.

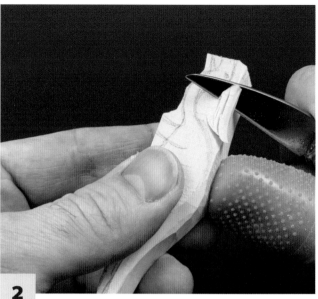

2 **Carve out the material above the head and neck.** Use a V-cut to remove the wood, starting with a knife stroke from the head and meeting that cut with a knife stroke from the body. Continue expanding the V with paring or push cuts from both sides until there's a curved dip that almost reaches the boundary on the pattern.

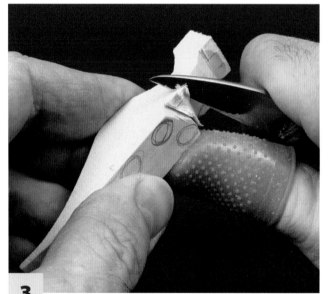

3 **Establish the leg area.** Draw footprints on the bottom of the wood. Using stop cuts, carve in front of the front legs and behind the back legs. With the first knife stroke, make a stop cut at the boundary of the feet and match that with a knife stroke from the neck. Repeat on the back legs with knife strokes on the boundary of the back of the feet and matching second strokes from the tail area. Continue to remove material with repeated stop cuts until you nearly reach the drawn boundaries.

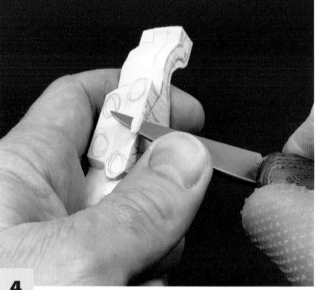

4 **Separate the front legs from the back legs.** Using V-cuts, remove material from between the front and back legs. Repeat until you reach the boundary of the belly, then use stop cuts to establish the boundary with the legs. With the first knife strokes, establish the edge of the legs and meet that cut with knife strokes from the belly. Round the edges of the belly with paring cuts.

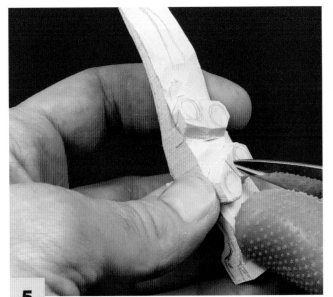

5 **Separate the left legs from the right legs.** Using the tip of the knife blade, make a pair of cuts that achieve a V-shaped groove between the left and right legs on both the front and rear pairs. Continue to expand this groove with paring or push cuts that meet at the deepest point of the groove. When the groove reaches the belly, switch to stop cuts. Use the boundary of the footprint as a guide as you make cuts along the inside of the leg. Meet those cuts with knife strokes that are flush with the surface of the belly. Round the boundary of the legs with push cuts toward the belly, leaving some extra material for strength.

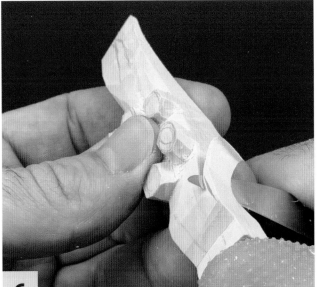

6 **Narrow the head and neck.** Using push or paring cuts, remove material from both sides of the head and neck, leaving extra material to be removed later. Where the neck connects to the head may be particularly weak, so be careful as you carve not to put unnecessary pressure on that area. Remove small amounts with each knife stroke rather than trying to remove all of the material in one stroke.

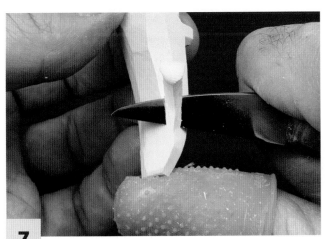

7 **Start the tail.** Draw the midpoint of the tail from above, giving it a slight curve at the tip. Remove the material from the sides of the tail using paring or push cuts. Where the tail curves, use shallow V-cuts, starting with knife strokes beginning near the tip of the tail and meeting them with strokes from the other direction. This will help keep the tip from snapping off. Round the edges of the tail and back with push or paring cuts, but leave extra material to be removed later.

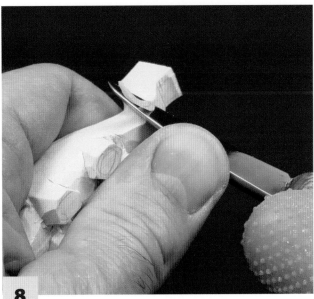

8 **Carve the neck.** Narrow the neck further, establishing the boundary with the head with V-cuts. With the first knife stroke starting at the back of the head, meet that cut with a cut from the neck toward the head. Pay special attention to the direction of the grain of the wood. If you are unsure, remove only small amounts of wood at a time to avoid putting too much pressure on the weak point.

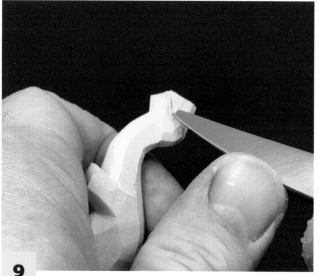

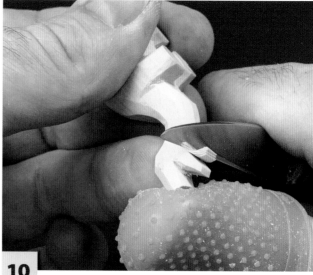

9 **Establish the mouth.** Draw the mouth on both sides of the head to use as a guide. Using just the tip of the blade, make two incisions on both sides of the head from the back of the mouth to the front. Angle the blade slightly toward the middle of the gap you wish to make so that the triangular chip is removed. Continue to expand the gap with the tip of the knife until the two notches meet in the middle.

10 **Refine the head.** Using push or paring cuts, remove material from above the top jaw and smooth with the edges at the front of the jaw. Using stop cuts, thin the bottom jaw. Start the first knife stroke at the tip of the lower jaw and cut toward the neck. Match this stroke with a stroke from the neck that slices off the material. Use push or paring cuts to smooth the edges of the outside of the lower jaw. Be careful to not use too much force.

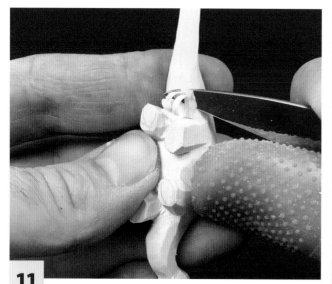

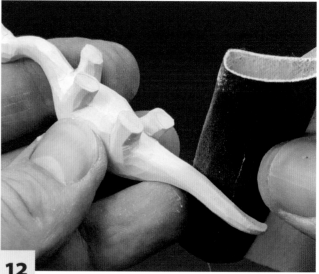

11 **Make final refinements to the legs, neck, and tail.** Look over the entire figure and use small paring or push cuts to smooth edges. Narrow the tail and neck to their final dimensions using paring or push cuts. Thin the legs with paring cuts from the footprints toward the belly and chop off the material with cuts at the base of each leg, flush with the surface of the belly.

12 **Sand.** Start with a coarse (200–400-grit) sandpaper, being careful around the head, neck, and tail so as not to remove too much material. Follow this with a finer (600–800-grit) sandpaper to achieve a smooth surface over the entire carving. (If you wish to have a faceted, rough look, ignore this part of the step.) Now look over the entire figure to clean up any transitions or surfaces that look rough. Finally, drill a 1/16" (1.6mm) hole in the bottom of the figure and insert a toothpick to hold while painting.

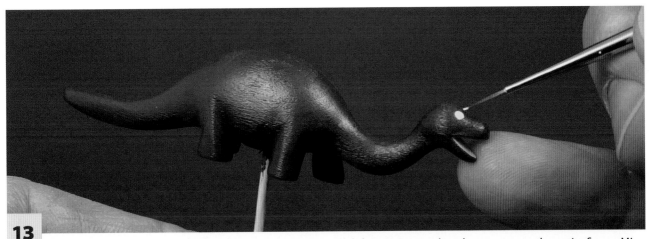

13 **Start painting.** Mix blue, yellow, and red paint to create a dark forest green and apply two coats to the entire figure. Mix red, white, and yellow to create a pink color. Apply one coat to the mouth. Mix yellow and white and use this color to paint the eyes. Add black for each pupil and white for each reflection.

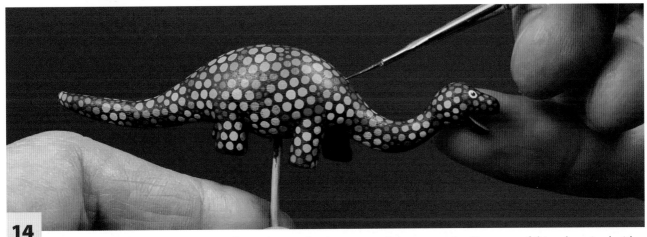

14 **Paint the scale pattern.** Mix blue, yellow, white, and red to create a light green color. Use some of this color mixed with white and yellow to make four more shades of green progressively lighter than the first. Paint an evenly distanced pattern of dots with the lightest green, surround those dots with a ring of dots from the next darkest shade, and repeat with progressively darker shades until the circles of dots meet. Use the darkest of the light greens to fill in the blank areas with dots.

Pattern

Leaping Pig

From delicious to dirty, pigs have played a large, complex role in human history, culture, and cuisine since being domesticated more than 10,000 years ago. In Germany, the "Gluck Schwein" or lucky pig is a popular charm in gifts and greeting cards, so it's a natural subject for the artist entrepreneur. Some of my favorite images are the leaping pig paintings of Michael Sowa; I made a design that approximates that pose. Adding a simple set of wings transforms it into the famous and unlikely flying pig; the Flugschwein is equally at home elevated from its pedestal with a toothpick as it is hanging from a twig.

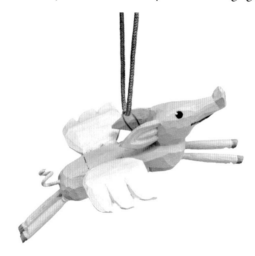

Materials & Tools

- Wood: ⅝" x ⁷⁄₁₆" x 1⅝" (1.6 x 1.1 x 4.1cm), grain running in the longest dimensions
- Several toothpicks
- 1" (2.5cm) piece of bendable wire
- Carving knife
- Hand protection
- Pin vise with ¹⁄₁₆" (1.6mm) drill bit
- Wood glue
- Super glue
- Sandpaper: 200–400 grit and 600–800 grit
- Paintbrushes: #1 or larger round paintbrush, #10/0 liner or smaller detail brush
- Paints: red, yellow, white, and black to mix shades of light peach, gray, and peach-tinted cream

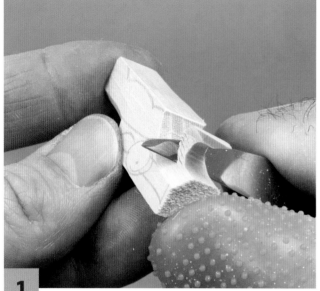

1 **Rough out.** Transfer the pattern (without legs) to the wood. Rough out the basic form by removing the wood on opposite corners with a series of paring or push cuts. Start on the edges about one-third the distance from the ends and carve out to almost halfway through the piece below the chin and above the body behind the ears.

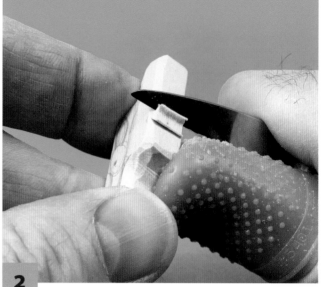

2 **Carve the belly.** Soften the edges of the body section with paring or push cuts on the back, bottom, and rear. Establish the belly using two sets of multiple V-cuts on the bottom of the body section near the front and rear. The first strokes should begin nearest the ends and be directed toward the middle. The knife strokes that chip out the wood should start closest to the middle of the belly and be directed toward the front and rear. Blend the V-shaped notches in front and behind the belly with the sides of the body using long, sweeping paring cuts.

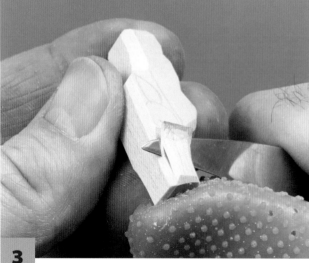

3 **Narrow the snout.** Use paring or push cuts directed from the head toward the nostrils. Remove about one-quarter of the material from each side and smooth the edges of the nose both top and bottom. Establish the ridge at the tip of the nose with a V-cut beginning with a knife stroke that starts near the tip and is directed toward the head. Carve out the wood with a stroke from the forehead directed toward the nose. Give the ridge more definition with a second set of more acute V-cuts. To avoid carving off the nose ridge, always make the first stroke toward the head.

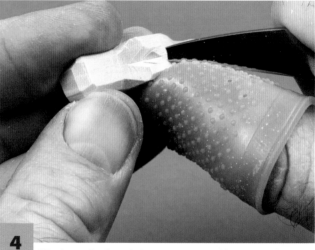

4 **Work on the head.** Remove material between the ears and behind the back of the head. Start with a V-cut between the ears from above, then expand and broaden the gap by repeating three-stroke combination cuts in the same location. The first two knife strokes should match and expand the initial groove; with the third stroke, use the tip of the knife across the back of the head to chip out the wood.

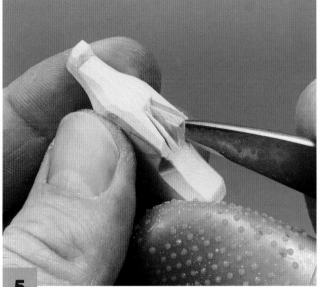

5 **Continue between the ears.** Widen and deepen the gap between the ears with push and paring cuts. Repeat until the groove is expanded downward to meet the back of the body. Make push cuts on one ear and paring cuts on the other. Direct the cuts so that the ears are thinner at the tips than at the base, where the ears should stay about ³⁄₃₂" (2.4mm) thick. Where the material is still connected to the body, chip it out using knife strokes that are flush with the top of the pig's back.

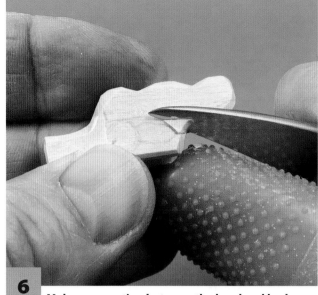

6 **Make a separation between the head and body.** Make paring cuts on the top of each ear from the middle of the ear to the tip. Make V-cuts where the ear connects to the top of the head. Cut a V-shaped groove between the head and body. Use a V-cut between the tip of the ear and the body. On the bottom of the ear where it connects to the head, make a three-stroke combination cut that chips out a small, triangular piece of wood.

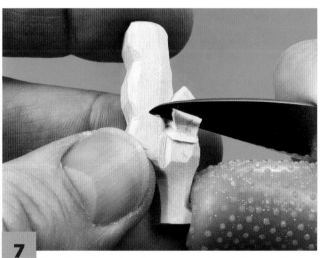

7 **Continue forming the ears and head.** Narrow the ear from the outside with V-cuts that end at the head, making sure to keep the ear thick enough that it is still stable. Blend this groove with the head using paring cuts. Smooth the angled edges on the side and top of the head. Narrow the head in front of the ear and blend it into the snout with paring cuts.

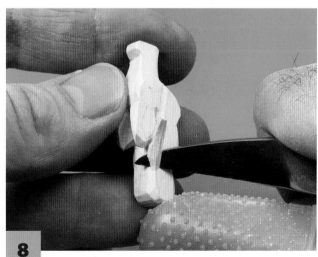

8 **Continue shaping the ears.** Separate the bottom of the ear from the back of the body with narrow V-shaped grooves. Expand the grooves with repetition deeper under the ear until separation occurs. Thin the bottom inside of the ears with push cuts that create bevels on the bottom edges of the ears. Be careful to avoid contacting the back of the body with the knife tip.

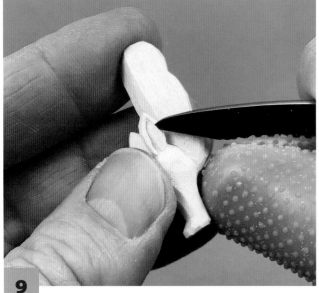

9

Add ear detail. Incise the outside of each ear with leaf-shaped patterns that match the shape of the ears. Using the tip of the knife like a pencil, carve the shallow V-shaped groove about 1⁄16" (1.6mm) from the edges of the ear. Make each groove in two strokes. Avoid pushing too deep—just go halfway through the ear. Chip out the material at the base of the head using the tip of the knife stroke flush with the head.

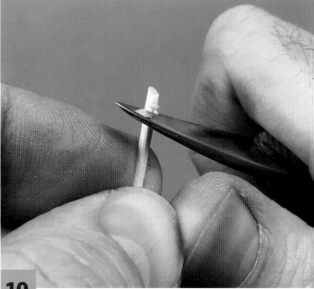

10

Make four legs out of toothpicks. You can use one toothpick to make two legs. For each leg, chop the toothpick diagonally and establish the hoof with a notch using a V-cut about 1⁄16" (1.6mm) in from the short side of the diagonal cut. Make the first knife stroke nearest the hoof and meet it with a stroke from the opposite direction. About 3⁄4" (1.9cm) in from the hoof, make a series of cuts around the circumference of the toothpick to make a 1⁄8" (3.2mm)–long taper, then chop off the leg at the thinnest part of the taper.

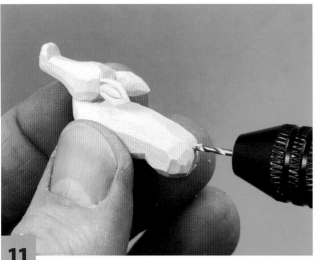

11

Add the legs and tail. Drill six 1⁄16" (1.6mm) holes: four for the legs, one for the tail, and one on the belly to insert a toothpick for holding while painting. Apply wood glue to the tapered ends of the legs and insert them so that the hooves are correctly oriented. Bend a piece of wire approximately 5⁄8" (1.6cm) long around a toothpick to make a curly tail. Apply super glue to the wire, insert it into the tail hole, and wedge it in place with the sharpened end of a toothpick.

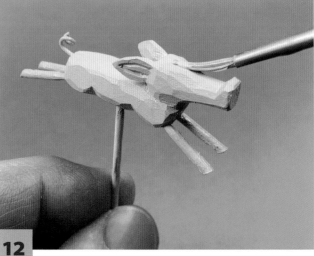

12

Paint pink all over. Mix white, red, and yellow paint to get a light peach color. Some red paints dry darker than they appear when wet, which will make a skin tone more pink than peach. To remedy this, make sure the color you've mixed is a very light peach shade when wet. Apply two coats of paint over the entire figure. After you've let the first coat dry, examine the color in natural light to determine if the color needs to be adjusted lighter for the second coat.

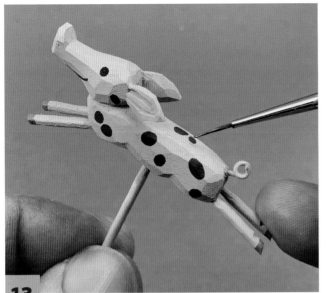

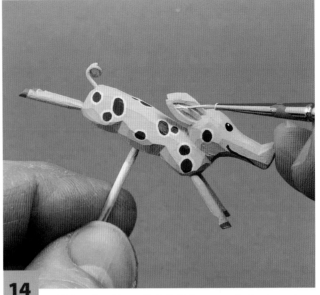

13 **Add features and dots.** Pencil in dots for the eyes before you paint them to ensure that they are evenly spaced and symmetrical. Paint the eyes black. The eyes can be round or oval; either way, use a circular motion to spread the paint evenly. Pencil in the mouth, then apply a light to medium gray (mixed from black and white) for the mouth and hooves. Use a darker gray to paint random jellybean-shaped dots of various sizes on the body.

14 **Add details .** Mix a slightly lighter peach shade and mix in a touch of gray. Outline the gray jellybean shapes on the body; paint the inside of the ear as well. Outlining can be a difficult but effective technique; it accentuates features and makes them pop. Relax and pay attention to your breathing as if you are meditating to make it easier. Finally, make a white reflection dot in each eye.

When Pigs Fly

To make the flying version of the pig, follow the same pattern until step 9, then carve and attach the wings. Using a piece of wood that is 1½" x ½" x ⅛" (3.8cm x 1.3cm x 3.2mm) with the grain running in the long direction, make three sets of shallow V-cuts to establish the gull shape of the wing, then use paring cuts to narrow the ends. Draw the outline of the wing and use the tip of the blade to carve the feather points. Use V-cuts to establish the curves at the front and back of the wings where they'll meet the body and square off a middle section to make it about ¼" (6.4mm) wide. Transfer the measurement for the length of that middle section to the top of the pig body and use stop cuts to excavate a squared-off notch to accept the wing. Glue the wing in place and continue assembling the pig from step 10. For the hanger, drill a 1/16" (1.6mm) hole on the back of the pig between the ears and secure a loop of flexible wire by gluing and wedging it into place with the point of a toothpick, which can then be snapped off.

Patterns

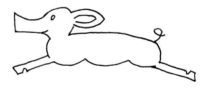

Leaping Goat

Goats have a delightful character, a disregard for barriers, and an easygoing palate; in a way, they are good role models for kids, and not just goat kids. The paintings of artist Marc Chagall are filled with poetic symbolism often containing goat imagery that could be used as a springboard for ideas. For this project, I've chosen an endangered heritage breed from where I live, the Thüringenlandziege. It's just a rough approximation, a jumping off point for the design and painting. Adding a few rouge colors to a rich brown coat gives the carving more vitality. Like so much of my carving and painting, it's not a literal representation, but rather a whimsical deviation from reality.

Materials & Tools

- Wood: ⅜" x ⅞" x 1⅜" (1 x 2.2 x 3.5cm), grain running in the longest dimension
- Several toothpicks
- Carving knife
- Hand protection
- Pin vise with ¹⁄₁₆" (1.6mm) and ¹⁄₃₂" (0.8mm) drill bits
- Sandpaper: 400–600 grit
- Paintbrushes: #1 or larger round paintbrush, #10/0 liner or smaller detail brush
- Paints: red, blue, yellow, white, and black to mix shades of brown and gray

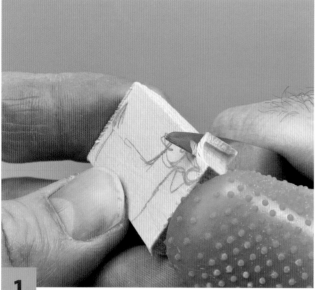

1 **Rough out.** Transfer the pattern (without legs) to the wood. Rough out above and below the head. Use paring or push cuts to remove material from above the head and nose. Start with knife strokes at the forehead and slice in the direction of the nose. Use paring or push cuts to remove material from under the head. You'll be cutting mostly across the grain, so it will require extra strength. Remove just small amounts of wood with each stroke.

2 **Define the beard.** Use stop cuts to establish the outline of the beard. Make the first knife strokes flush with the neck and match those with strokes starting at the tip of the beard and proceeding toward the neck. Leave plenty of extra material to remove later; the beard is not flowing in the direction of the grain and is therefore one of the weakest points in the carving.

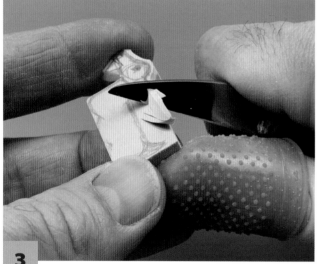

3 **Rough out behind the head.** Use paring cuts to remove material above the ears and V-cuts to remove the material above the back between the tail and the neck. Preserve material for the ears. Start with knife strokes from the tail in the direction of the head and match those with strokes from the head toward the tail so as not to snap off the tail accidentally. Excavate the area to the top of the body, then use knife strokes that slice flush with the back to meet cuts made from the tail and neck.

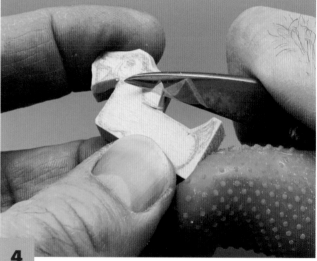

4 **Define the bottom edges of the ears.** Use stop cuts under the ear and behind the neck to help establish the ears. Make the first cuts flush with the back and meet them with knife strokes from the tip of the ears. Make another series of stop cuts, this time making the first knife stroke along the lower edge of the ear. For the second knife stroke, use the tip of the knife starting at the base of the ear to slice out the material immediately under the ear. Extend the valley from both sides until they meet in the middle.

5 **Round and define the body.** Use paring or push cuts to round the edges of the body, then use V-cuts to establish the dips that will separate the belly area from the base areas of the front and rear legs. Start with knife strokes from the front and rear toward the middle and match those with knife strokes from the belly directed toward the two ends. Round the edges of these curves with paring or push cuts.

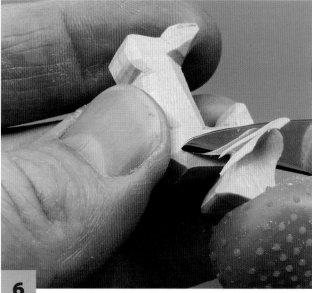

6 **Narrow the head, beard, neck, and tail.** Using push or paring cuts, narrow the head, starting each knife stroke at the base of an ear and slicing toward the nose. Using stop cuts, make the neck thinner than the head. Make the first cuts at the cheeks, running from a little below the base of the ear all the way to the nose. Meet these cuts with a knife stroke that begins where the neck and body meet and proceeds in the direction of the head. Narrow the tail with a series of paring or push cuts that start at the top tip of the tail and are directed toward the body. Chip out this material with cuts that are flush with the back.

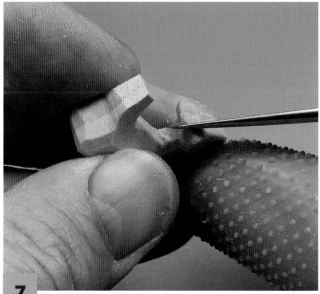

7 **Separate the left and right ears.** Start with a V-cut on the top of the ear region to establish a groove. Expand the groove with paring or push cuts with the tip of the blade that start in the groove and are directed toward the tip of each ear. Extend the gap downward between the ears with a series of push cuts on the backsides of the ears. Fashion the ears so that they angle outwards slightly. Keep them extra thick to retain strength; they will be refined later.

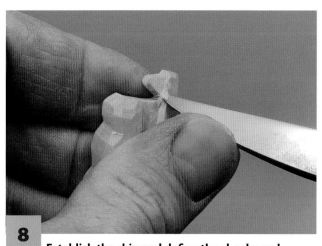

8 **Establish the chin and define the cheeks and beard.** Use the tip of the blade to make combination cuts that establish a shallow dip behind the chin. Start the first knife stroke under the chin and cut toward the neck. Start the second knife stroke at the jaw line and meet the first cut, then slice out the material with a third cut that runs flush with the beard. Use paring cuts to narrow the beard and round the front and back edges, but leave it thicker in the middle.

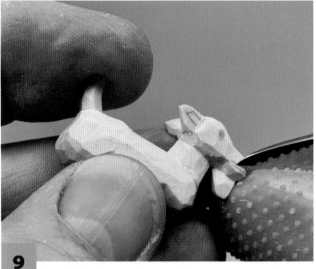

9 **Establish the mouth and define the inside of the ears.** Draw a line for the mouth and a V for the inside of the ear to use as guides. For the mouth, use the tip of the knife to make a pair of incisions that meet, making a groove along the guideline. For the ear, make a three-stroke combination cut using the tip of the blade. Start with two shallow incisions starting near the tip of the ear and running to the base of the ear in the form of a V. Make a third incision at the base of the ear connecting the first two incisions to chip out the wood.

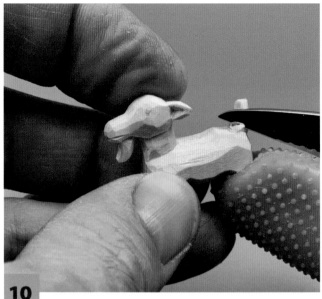

10 **Refine the tail.** Using paring cuts, narrow and round the tail. Since the tail has short grain, it will be rather weak, so be careful not to snap it off as you carve. Start your knife strokes near the tip and make it pointy before narrowing the tail where it connects to the body. Cut across the grain and toward the body. Clean up the area around the base with controlled cuts that run flush with the body.

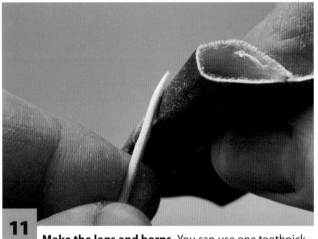

11 **Make the legs and horns.** You can use one toothpick to make two legs. For each leg, chop the toothpick diagonally and establish the hoof with a notch using a V-cut about ¹⁄₁₆" (1.6mm) in from the short side of the diagonal cut. Make the first knife stroke nearest the hoof and meet it with a stroke from the opposite direction. About ¾" (1.9cm) in from the hoof, make a series of cuts around the circumference of the toothpick to make a ⅛" (3.2mm)–long taper, then chop off the leg at the thinnest part of the taper. For each horn, chop a toothpick at a 60-degree angle (rather than the 45-degree diagonal cut for the hooves), then use 400–600-grit sandpaper to shape the end into a horn shape.

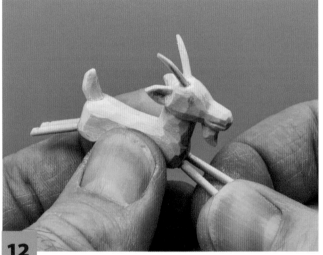

12 **Refine the figure and insert horns and legs.** Drill ¹⁄₃₂" (0.8mm) starter holes for the horns to avoid tearing, then drill seven ¹⁄₁₆" (1.6mm) holes: two for the horns, four for the legs, and one on the belly to insert a toothpick for holding while painting. Use paring cuts to narrow the body to within ¹⁄₃₂" (0.8mm) of the leg holes. Look over the entire figure; blend and soften the lines with paring cuts wherever needed and see that everything is symmetrical. Glue the legs and horns into the holes with wood glue. Use 400–600-grit sandpaper to refine the shape of the horns as needed.

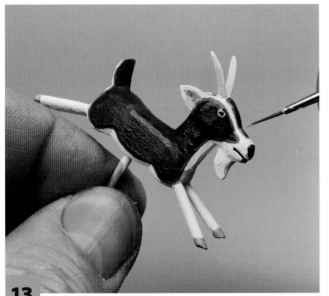

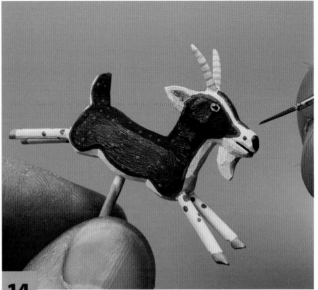

13 **Start painting.** Mix red, yellow, and a touch of both blue and white to create a dark reddish brown color and apply this to the back, neck, and head of the figure as shown. Add white paint to the mixture and use this color to outline the dark area. Paint black oval eyes. Mix yellow with a touch of red and white to create an amber color to paint the irises. Mix black, white, and a touch of yellow to create a taupe color; apply this to the hooves. Finally, paint a white dot in each pupil.

14 **Add details.** Inspired by a real goat breed, I decided to lighten the dark field of color with some lighter browns—one leaning red, the other yellow. Mix the three primary colors and white in the correct amounts to achieve your brown hues. Apply the darker, reddish brown in an ordered, hair-like pattern; apply the lighter golden brown as dots between the hair and as speckles on the upper legs.

A Fanciful Variation

If you want to take your goat further into the fantasy realm, paint the coat with flowers on a field of green. Mounting the goat on a base will make it appear as if its leap is frozen in midair. For display purposes, this is a simple and effective way to present a dynamic pose. Use a colorful, figured piece of wood that is 1¼" x ⅞" x ⅜" (3.1 x 2.2 x 1cm). Drill a ¹⁄₁₆" (1.6mm) hole in the middle of the block. Paint a toothpick black and insert one end into the block and the other into the hole in the bottom of the carving.

Pattern

Leaping Leopard

Big cats move through the world with a quiet power as a living embodiment of beauty. They're legendary predators; they elicit in us a primitive fear. I once came face-to-face with a roaring mountain lion; luckily, my bladder was empty! I found out seconds later it had been rescued as a kitten and bottlefed since birth, so it was tame as a tabby, yet still it possessed an unnerving intensity. If you have a cat in the house, you've already got a small model of the big cats to study. The paintings of Henri Rousseau are useful as well, especially if you want to plan a diorama around the figure. This leopard carving features a simplified design for the characteristic pouncing of an ambush predator.

Materials & Tools

- Wood: ⅜" x ⅝" x 1⅝" (1 x 1.6 x 4.1cm), grain running in the longest dimension
- Several toothpicks
- Carving knife
- Detail knife (optional)
- Hand protection

- Pin vise with 1⁄16" (1.6mm) drill bit
- Paintbrushes: #1 or larger round paintbrush, #10/0 liner or smaller detail brush
- Paints: red, blue, yellow, white, and black to mix shades of light orange

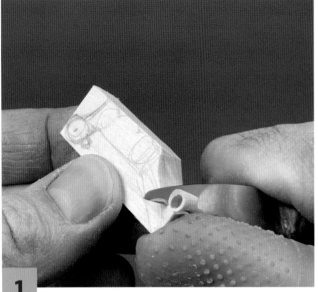

1 **Rough out.** Transfer the pattern (without legs) to the wood. Use paring or push cuts to remove the material from below the tail. Don't carve all the way to the lines—leave a little extra to carve away later. You'll be using the tail to hold onto the carving, so it needs to have more girth than the finished piece.

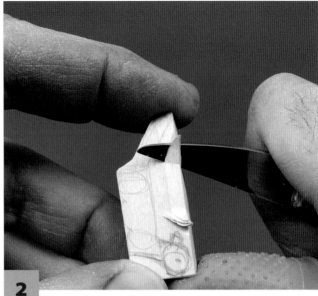

2 **Work on the back.** Make stop cuts at the top of the figure to remove material from the tips of the ears to the tip of the tail. The first cut should be made behind the ears and be met or matched with knife strokes coming from the direction of the tail. Continue with repeated stop cuts in the same location until the excavation reaches the boundary with the body.

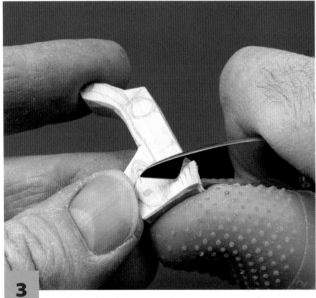

3 **Work on the chest area.** Use paring or push cuts to remove material from under the chin, in front of the neck and body. Start knife strokes at the base of the chest and slice toward the nose. Repeat until you've scooped out the material from in front of the body. Leave extra material for the nose to be refined later.

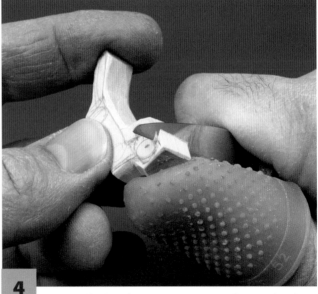

4 **Narrow the head.** Using paring or push cuts, slice from the forehead to the nose. Also narrow the sides of the head. Start the knife strokes at the ear region and gradually taper the profile until you reach the nose.

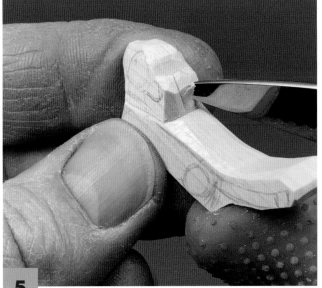

5 **Separate the ears.** Use a V-cut from above to begin separating the ears. Expand the wedge shape with repeated knife strokes until it reaches the back of the head. Make stop cuts directly in the middle of the wedge, flush with the head in the direction of each ear. Meet these stop cuts with knife strokes on the backside of each ear. A smaller detail knife is helpful when cutting inside these tight spaces, but the tip of a larger blade will also work.

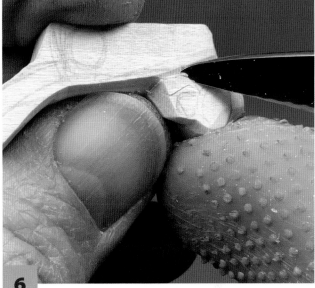

6 **Define the ears from the bottom up.** Make a three-stroke combination cut below the ears and behind the neck. Use the tip of the blade as you make two matched cuts deep into the wood beneath the ear. The bottom knife stroke should slice flush with the body; the top stroke follows the bottom of the ear; and the third cut connects the first two and chips out the wood. Finish the curve at bottom edge of the ear with carefully considered paring and push cuts.

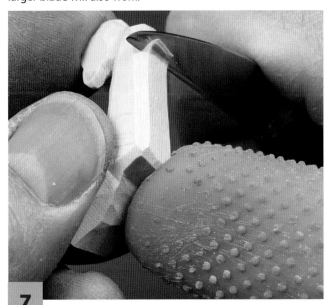

7 **Round the body.** Use paring or push cuts to smooth the angles of edges on the entire body. Use V-cuts on the bottom of the body in two places to establish the belly. Start with knife strokes from the front and rear toward the center. Meet the initial cuts with knife strokes from the opposite direction, starting at the belly and slicing toward each end.

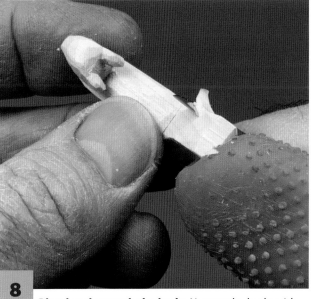

8 **Blend and smooth the body.** Narrow the body with paring and push cuts. Pare the wood on the back below the ears and cut off the resultant wood chip at the border with the neck. Look closely at the body from every angle and refine any sharp angles or asymmetry with more paring.

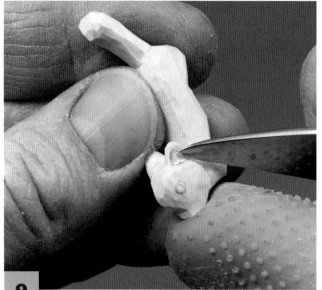

9 **Work on the features.** With a pencil, draw in the mouth and inside of ears as guides to follow. Using the tip of the blade, score the line that marks the mouth, then do this a second time but with the knife slightly angled. Still just using the tip of the blade, make a combination cut on the ears: cut into the guidelines and make sure to cut at angles that ensure the cuts meet at the center of the ear. Use a third stroke at the base of the ear to chip out the wood.

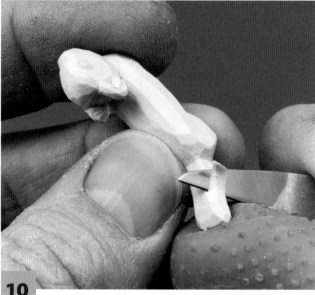

10 **Narrow the tail.** Look over the entire figure and clean up any messy transitions. Then narrow the smallest parts to their finished dimensions using paring or push cuts. Bring the tail to its final diameter and use long strokes to create the desired curve of the tail.

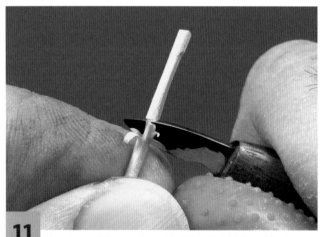

11 **Create and insert legs.** Drill five ¹⁄₁₆" (1.6mm) holes: four for the legs and one on the belly to insert a toothpick for holding while painting. Chop off the tapered end of a toothpick and make a pencil mark between ³⁄₈"–½" (1–1.3cm) from the end. Round the end with a series of cuts to form a paw. Make a stop cut ⅛" (3.2mm) from the end and meet it with a knife stroke that starts at the pencil mark. Make the back of the paw rounded at the stop cut with a couple paring cuts. Starting on the other side of the pencil mark, shave the toothpick into a graduated peg. Chop it off and insert it into the leg hole with wood glue.

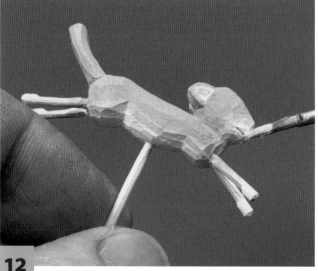

12 **Paint the base colors.** Mix red, yellow, and white paint to create a light orange/yellow color. Apply two coats to the tail, body, and head. Use white paint to coat the belly, inner ears, legs, and front of the neck and muzzle. While the paint is still wet, mix a portion of the yellow with the white to get a lighter orange and apply this color on the border between the orange and white areas; blend the border area to achieve a gradation of color.

13   **Paint the markings.** Use black paint to color the eyes, nose, mouth, whiskers, and ears. Start the leopard's dots at the forehead and continue down its back as rosette dot clusters that extend to the base of the tail. Paint black stripes or splotches on the tail. Mix red and yellow with a touch of white and blue to get an orange/brown color to apply to the middle of the rosettes. Add black dots to the legs. Finally, paint one white dot above each eye and another in each eye.

A Family of Felines

A jaguar (top) has closed rosettes with a dot in the middle of each one, but otherwise the painting and colors are the same as the leopard. A tiger (bottom) is painted much like the leopard too, except with stripes instead of rosettes. Start the stripes at the forehead and continue down the back to the tip of the tail, maintaining a constant style or finesse in the striping throughout. Add short stripes to the legs too, and a white area at the tip of the tail.

Pattern

Leaping Rabbit

We kept a pair of Castor Rex rabbits for a short while; their fur is velvety like a mole's. The buck made a habit of peeing on me, and my wife found this amusing until it happened to her! Despite the urinary shenanigans, rabbits are considered lucky animals; a severed foot can be a good luck charm to some people (who forget that it didn't work very well for the rabbit). Easter, on the other hand, makes the bunny a celebrity, so this project features a rabbit painted in Easter colors that makes a perfect accompaniment to colored eggs and chocolates. The trickiest part of any rabbit is the long, thin ears, which require constant diligence to keep them from breaking off, so this rabbit's ears are designed to run with the grain. Still, leave them relatively thick and undefined until everything else is nearly done.

Materials & Tools

- Wood: ⅜" x ⅝" x 1⅛" (1 x 1.6 x 2.9cm), grain running in the longest dimension
- Several toothpicks
- Carving knife
- Detail carving knife (optional)
- Hand protection

- Pin vise with 1⁄16" (1.6mm) drill bit
- Paintbrushes: #1 or larger round paintbrush, #10/0 liner or smaller detail brush
- Paints: red, blue, yellow, white, and black to mix shades of pink, yellow, and light blue

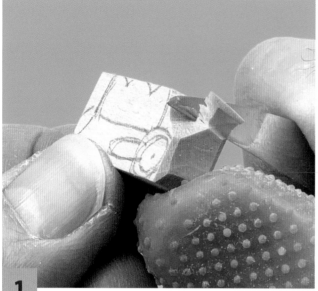

1

Rough out. Transfer the pattern (without legs) to the wood. Rough out the front and rear. Use paring or push cuts to take off material below the chin and tail. This will require that you carve nearly across the grain, so make sure your knife is sharp. Start by carving off the edges and corners. Don't carve all the way to the lines—leave a little extra material to remove later.

2

Remove material between the tail and ear tips. Using V-cuts, carve out to the back of the rabbit from behind the ears to the tail. Start with knife strokes from the tail directed toward the ears. Meet those cuts with strokes in the opposite direction, starting from the tip of the ears. Make stop cuts behind the ears and meet those cuts with knife strokes that slice parallel to the back of the body directed toward the ears.

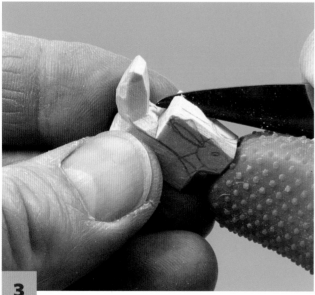

3

Divide the left and right ears. Draw two lines on the top of the figure to mark the ears; they should come out of the head angled slightly outward. Use V-cuts to make a separation between the left and right ears. Repeat the V-cuts until the groove has expanded to the insides of the ears and all the way to the back of the body.

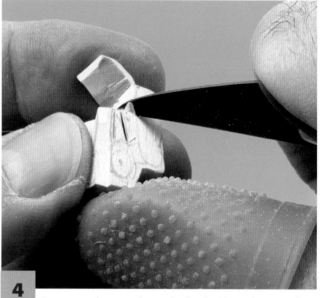

4

Separate the ears from the body. Use a three-stroke combination cut to chip out the material under the ears. Make one knife stroke flush with the body matched to another stoke flush with the bottom of the ear, directed at each other at a 45-degree angle. Use a third cut to connect the cuts at the back of the head and chop out the piece. Expand the groove deeper with repetition.

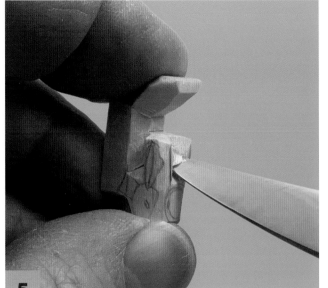

5 **Expand the gap between the ears.** Use push cuts on the back of the ears to create separation between them. Start with the knife tip at the center of the V-cut at the back of the head and slice toward the tip of the ear from the inside. Continue to use push cuts until you've connected this excavation with the space you created under the ears in the previous step.

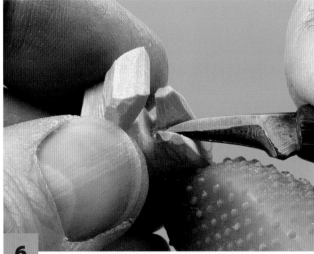

6 **Refine the ears.** Use stop cuts to remove material from between the ears. Narrow the ears and expand the gap between the ears where it connects to the head. Make the first knife strokes on the back of the ears directed toward the head. Meet these cuts with strokes running flush with the back of the head and neck to chop off the material. A small-bladed knife makes this easier. The Schnitzmesser (carving knife) pictured is a ⅝" (1.5cm)–long Wharncliffe form blade of Damascus steel made by a German knife maker, Peter Lucas.

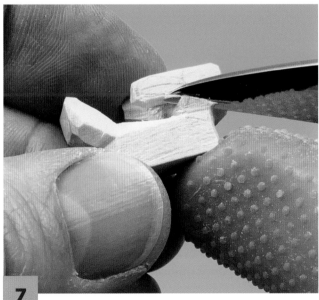

7 **Narrow the head.** Use paring or push cuts to remove material from the sides of the head. Start the knife stroke at the middle of the ear and slice toward the nose. Use V-cuts to establish the separation between the head and body. Make repeated shallow cuts until the neck is reached; don't make this area too thin.

8 **Round the head.** Use paring and push cuts to taper the side of the head; make the nose and mouth narrower than the back of the head. Make the edges of the head smoother with more paring knife strokes. Form the general look of the face. Use a pencil to try out eye locations, check for symmetry, and continue to whittle out the features as you desire. For the purposes of Easter decorations, the head can be either cartoonish or completely accurate.

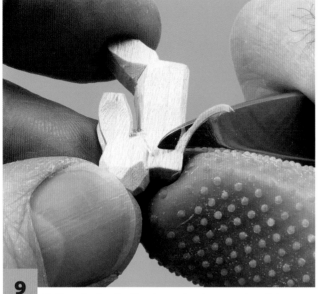

9   **Refine the body.** Cut down the sharp angles of the body with more paring or push cuts. Try to leave long, faceted knife marks on the wood, as this gives the impression of movement in the final piece. Make a set of V-cuts on each end of the belly. The first stroke of the knife should be at the ends of the body, directed toward the middle. Meet those cuts with strokes starting from the belly and directed toward the ends of the body.

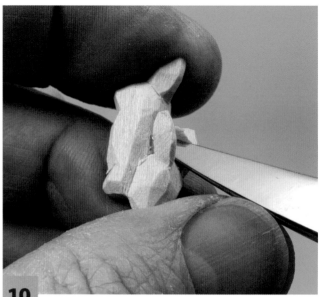

10   **Clean up the ears.** Using paring or push cuts, make the final refinements to each ear from the base to the tip. Start with the basic leaf-shaped outline, then switch to the backside of each ear, making the final touches with push cuts. Be careful with these last cuts. If you do break an ear, glue it with wood glue and let it dry overnight before you touch it again.

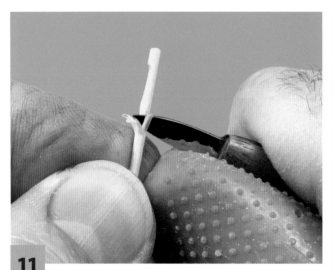

11   **Create and insert legs.** Drill five ¹⁄₁₆" (1.6mm) holes: four for the legs and one on the belly to insert a toothpick for holding while painting. Chop off the tapered end of a toothpick and make a pencil mark between ³⁄₈"–½" (1–1.3cm) from the end. Round the end with a series of cuts to form a paw. Make a stop cut ⅛" (3.2mm) from the end and meet it with a knife stroke that starts at the pencil mark. Make the back of the paw rounded at the stop cut with a couple paring cuts. Starting on the other side of the pencil mark, shave the toothpick into a graduated peg. Chop it off and insert it into the leg hole with wood glue.

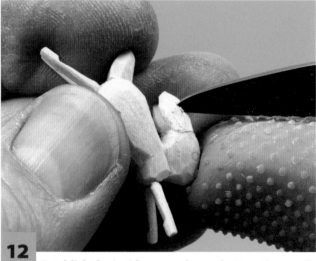

12   **Establish the inside ear and mouth.** Draw the mouth in with a pencil and make a V in each ear as guides for your blade. Using the tip of the blade, make a shallow cut along the pencil mark for the mouth and repeat at a slight angle to chip out a thin sliver of wood. Again using the tip of the blade, make a relatively shallow slicing knife stroke along each of the guidelines in the ear, with the cuts meeting in the middle along the length of the ear. Use a third cut at the base of the ear to chip out the wood.

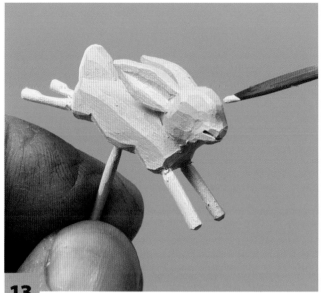

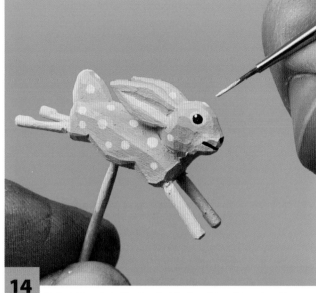

13 **Paint the base colors.** Select either blue, red, or yellow paint and add it to white to create a light pastel hue. Apply two coats to the body, head, and ears. Mix a little of this color with a larger quantity of white paint to create a tinted white hue. Apply two coats of this color to the belly, tail, legs, and insides of the ears as well as the front of the muzzle and neck. Mix the two hues together to create an in-between color and outline the border between the two color fields.

14 **Paint the details.** Apply black paint with a detail brush to create the eyes, nose, and mouth. Apply white paint to outline the eyes and paint in a dot for each eye reflection. Finally, apply white paint to make a random pattern of various sized small dots on the back and cheeks of the rabbit.

Cute Variations

Don't be afraid to make your carving look a little different from mine! Try a pointier or rounder face for your rabbit, a different tail angle, or a new color scheme, either whimsical or realistic.

Pattern

Leaping Horse

Horses are impressive beasts of burden with beauty and brawn and a brainpower equivalent to that of three-year-old humans. The power of horses carried humans for centuries, hence the word "horsepower," which is still used as a measure of mechanical strength today. From the cave paintings of Lascaux to Swedish Dala horses to Eadweard Muybridge's "The Horse in Motion," the equine form has inspired countless artists, both famous and anonymous. I've designed the form for this project with a simple cartoon style so you can concentrate on the head and ears. The finish I've chosen is a dapple-gray variant, but one search on the Internet will give you many other options to choose from. I've also included patterns for a unicorn and a Pegasus based on the same design, if you want to get more fantastical!

Materials & Tools

- Wood: ⅜" x ⅞" x 1¾" (1 x 2.2 x 4.5cm), grain running in the longest dimension
- Several toothpicks
- Carving knife
- Hand protection
- Pin vise with 1/16" (1.6mm) drill bit
- Paintbrushes: #1 or larger round paintbrush, #10/0 liner or smaller detail brush
- Paints: red, blue, yellow, white, and black to mix shades of gray

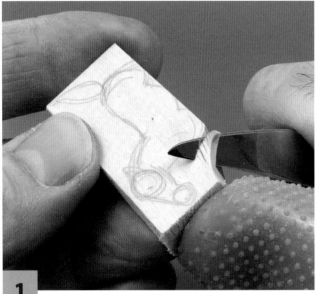

1 **Rough out.** Transfer the pattern (without legs) to the wood. Rough out the material below the head and below the tail, using paring or push cuts. The grain of the wood is running in the long direction, so these knife strokes will be slicing nearly across the grain; don't try to take off large chunks with each stroke, but rather use many cuts in repetition to achieve the desired excavation.

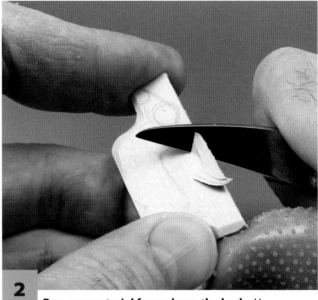

2 **Remove material from above the body.** Use repeated V-cuts to rough out the figure between the head and tail, starting with a knife stroke from the tail toward the head and matching it with a knife stroke from behind the head toward the tail. Leave enough material behind the head and neck for the ears. Once the repeated V-cuts have reached the top of the body of the horse, match the knife strokes from the head and tail with strokes that slice flush with the back.

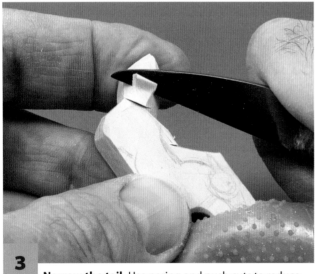

3 **Narrow the tail.** Use paring and push cuts to reduce the tail and round the edges. Where the tail meets the back, use stop cuts. Make the first knife strokes from the tail section and chip out the wood with strokes that slice flush with the back and meet the first cuts. Leave the transition from tail to body extra thick for now so that it doesn't snap off as you work on the rest of the figure.

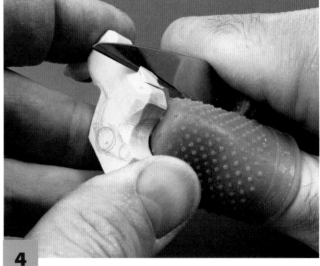

4 **Round the belly and start the nose.** Use paring or push cuts to round the edges of the belly, then use V-cuts to make the two dips that define the belly and separate it from the front and back areas of the body. Start with knife strokes from the ends and meet them with strokes from the belly section. Use paring or push cuts to remove the material from above the nose, starting at the forehead of the horse.

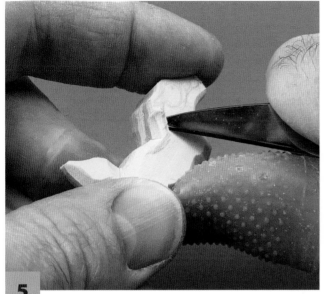

5 **Define the ears.** Use paring or push cuts to remove the material from behind the head above the ears. Also remove the material from behind the neck below the ears. Start the knife strokes at the tip of the ear and sweep downward toward the body. Chip out this material with a knife stroke slicing flush with the back of the horse.

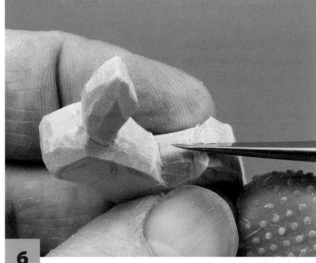

6 **Separate the left and right ears.** Using the tip of the knife, make a V-shaped groove with a pair of cuts running from the back of the head to the top of the back. Don't cut too deep—only about ¹⁄₁₆" (1.6mm). From above, use paring cuts to widen the groove to establish the backs of the ears and the border with the mane. Start with the knife tip in the groove and scoop out the material behind each ear. From under the ears, use stop cuts to establish the bottom edge and the border with the mane. Use the knife tip to slice at the ear's bottom boundary and chip out the material with a knife stroke using the knife tip from below to meet the cut.

7 **Define the features of the head and neck.** Use paring or push cuts to make the head and neck thinner and round the top edges of the head. Using stop cuts, define the separation between the head and neck; start with a knife stroke defining the border of the cheek and match that with a knife stroke starting at the transition between the body and the neck and slice toward the head.

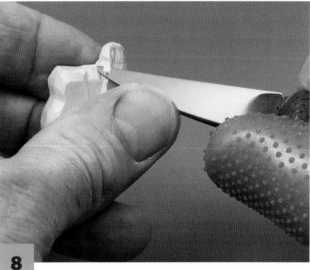

8 **Define the muzzle.** Using V-cuts, establish the chin bump under the mouth. Start with a knife stroke at the lowest point of the chin, slicing toward the neck. Match that with a knife stroke that starts where the head meets the neck. Round the front of the chin, top and bottom, with paring cuts. Use paring or push cuts to blend the cheeks with the area behind the chin.

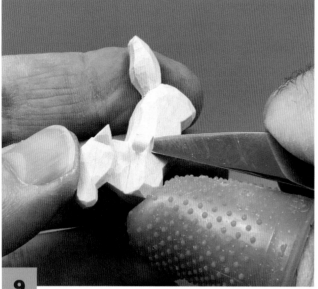

9 **Smooth the top and sides of the body.** Using paring and push cuts, round the edges on the back of the horse and remove material from the middle of the back to create the rump. Use stop cuts at the borders of the back with the neck and mane and with the back and tail. For the transition with the neck, the first knife strokes can be from either area, but when working on the border with the tail, always make the first cut on the tail section and match with one from the body to avoid breakage.

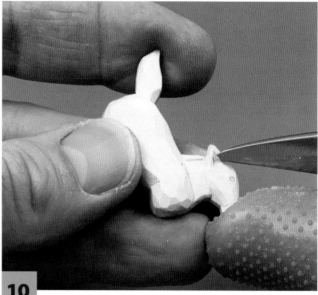

10 **Detail the mouth and ears.** Draw the mouth on the wood and a sideways V shape in each ear to use as guides. Using the tip of the knife, make a V-shaped groove by matching shallow incised cuts following the guideline for the mouth. Use the tip to make two more shallow incisions following the guidelines in each ear, then match those cuts with a third at the base of each ear, chipping out a triangular pyramid-shaped piece of wood.

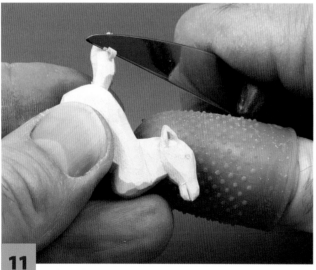

11 **Refine the tail.** The transition from the tail to the body has the shortest grain of the whole figure, so it will be the weakest and should be completed last. Use paring and push cuts to complete work on the end of the tail first, working your way toward the body. Use paring cuts on the top of the tail and push cuts underneath to follow the grain of the wood. Soften the curves of the tail so that it looks like it's flowing by using knife strokes to make long facets.

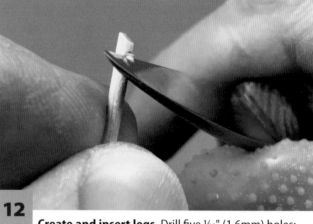

12 **Create and insert legs.** Drill five ⅟₁₆" (1.6mm) holes: four for the legs and one on the belly to insert a toothpick for holding while painting. For each leg, chop a toothpick diagonally at a 30-degree angle and establish the hoof with a notch using a V-cut about ⅟₁₆" (1.6mm) in from the short side of the diagonal cut. Make the first knife stroke nearest the hoof and meet it with a stroke from the opposite direction. About ⅝" (1.6cm) in from the hoof, make a series of cuts around the circumference of the toothpick to make a ⅛" (3.2mm)–long taper, then chop off the leg at the thinnest part of the taper. Insert the four legs into the leg holes with wood glue.

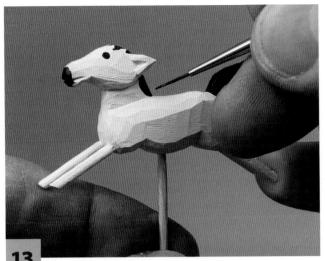

13 **Paint the base colors.** Apply two coats of white paint to the entire horse. If the paint reveals areas of the horse that need more work—fuzzy transitions, for instance—use a knife to clean up the affected area and apply white paint over the top. Draw eyes with a pencil, making sure they are symmetrical, and apply black paint to the tail, mane, nose, and eyes.

14 **Paint the details.** Mix black and white paint to create a medium gray color. Paint irregular areas of gray on the body and neck of the figure. Lighten the gray mix with white and roughly outline the gray areas and the nose. Lighten this gray mix again and apply another rough outline to the outside of the gray areas, nose, and eyes. Apply tiny white dots to the gray fields and a single white dot to each eye. Mix the light gray with a touch of yellow to create a light taupe color and apply it to the hooves.

Magical Variations

To make a unicorn (left), simply add a goatee and horn to your horse. Make the horn from the tapered end of a toothpick approximately ⅝" (1.6cm) long. Taper the other end to fit a 1/16" (1.6mm) hole drilled in the head. Use fine sandpaper (600–800 grit) to fine-tune the taper and glue into place. To make a flying Pegasus (right), follow the instructions for the flying pig variation in the Leaping Pig project.

Patterns

Miniature: Frog

We all casually conspire with the English language, convinced that "huge" equates with "important" while tiny things are belittled. It's a vestige of an era before microscopic electronics ran everything. Big things are grand, but miniatures have always been precious and intrinsically artistic. Like a compressed spring, a frog is loaded with exquisite power to leap despite a shockingly fragile appearance; they're paradigms of puny. When carving something small like this, a deft hand and practiced knowledge of the material is needed to apply just the right amount of force. Roughing out is quick; the devil is in the details. Smaller works are more difficult to handle. If you can, design them to be carved at the end of a larger piece of wood and leave them attached until you're nearly finished.

Materials & Tools

- Basswood: ½" x ½" x 1½" (1.3 x 1.3 x 3.8cm), grain running in the longest dimension
- 1 toothpick
- Carving knife
- Detail knife (optional)
- Hand protection
- Pin vise with ¹⁄₁₆" (1.6mm) drill bit
- Paintbrushes: #1 or larger round paintbrush, #10/0 liner or smaller detail brush
- Paints: blue, yellow, white, and black to mix shades of blue

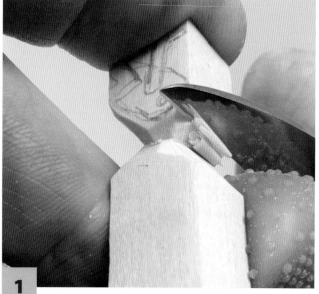

1 **Define the carving area.** Transfer the pattern to the wood. Draw the footprints of the frog on the end of the piece. Use a series of V-cuts around the circumference of the block to make a boundary establishing the top of the frog's head and body. Leave enough material connected so that the frog doesn't break off. Leave it attached until the carving is nearly complete.

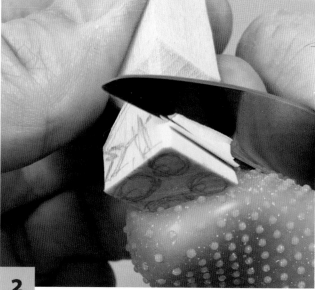

2 **Rough out.** Use V-cuts to rough out the front part of the frog by removing material from under the chin in front of the front legs. With the first knife strokes, establish a boundary above the feet. Start the second strokes below the chin and chip out the material from above. Leave the foot area thick for now so that it does not break in the process of carving the rest of the figure.

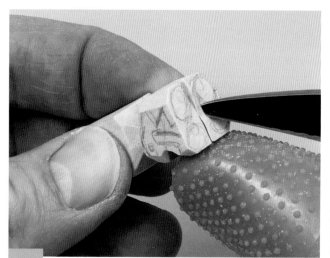

3 **Start separating the feet.** Begin to build a separation between all four feet. Using the tip of the knife like a pencil, make paired strokes to incise two narrow grooves that intersect in the middle of the four feet. Repeat the cuts to deepen the grooves. Use the footprints on the bottom of the figure as a guide for where not to cut.

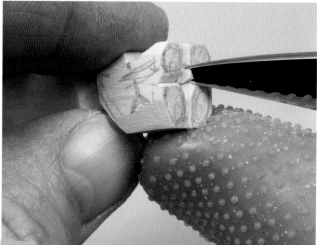

4 **Continue separating the feet.** Expand the excavation where the two incised grooves cross by making four cuts that produce a diamond-shaped notch in the middle of the four feet. Use the tip of the knife to further expand the grooves and round the corners of the footprints. You'll be cutting into the grain at an unusual angle, but if the wood is soft and your blade is sharp, it should be easy; if it's hard, take off less material with each stroke. Repeat the cuts until the separation has been expanded to the boundaries of the feet.

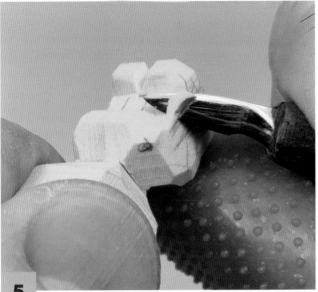

5 **Work on the legs.** Start to separate the front of the front legs left from right with incised grooves using the tip of the knife. Narrow the front legs with knife strokes that start at the top of the feet and end where the legs meet the body. Chip out the material with secondary knife strokes running flush with the underside of the body to establish the boundary of the belly of the frog.

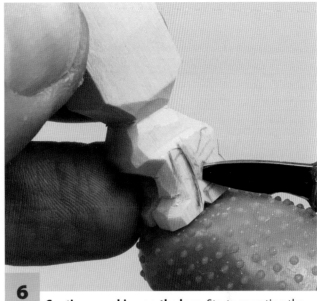

6 **Continue working on the legs.** Start separating the front from the back legs with incised grooves using the tip of the knife. Hold the knife like a pencil and make a pair of knife strokes on each side that meet, creating a V-shaped groove. Widen and deepen the grooves with repeated knife strokes on both sides until you reach the body of the frog. Be careful not to contact the feet with the knife.

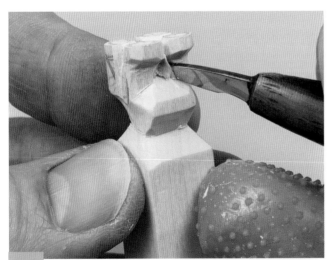

7 **Clear the belly area.** Widen the gap between the left and right legs on both the front and back sets of legs. With the first strokes, start near the feet and cut upward toward the belly. Chip out the material with the next stroke by cutting flush with the belly of the frog. Repeat until the area under the belly is cleared of material.

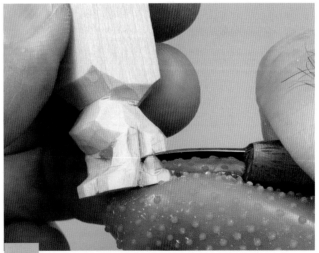

8 **Establish the rear feet using stop cuts.** From the gap between the legs, make a cut over the top of the foot and match that with a knife stroke directed from the knee to the foot, chipping out the material. Continue to deepen the notch with repeated stop cuts until the rear feet are established. Leave the feet somewhat thick until later to resist breakage. When making the knife stroke from the knee to the foot, be sure not to cut off the foot.

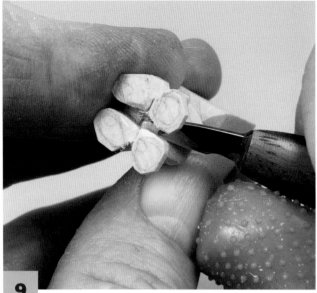

9 **Finish the legs.** Clear out the material between the left and right legs both front and back by making stop cuts. Trim the insides of the legs with knife strokes that start near the feet and proceed upward toward the belly; remove the resultant chip with a knife stroke that is flush with the belly. A detail knife is useful in these confined spaces. Expand the gap under the belly until the insides of the legs are even with the outside of the body.

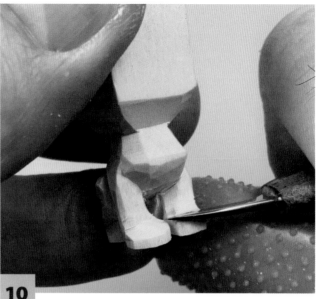

10 **Shape and thin the feet.** Use paring cuts to cut across the grain on top of the feet and paring cuts with the grain around the entire perimeter of the footprint. Smooth the edges of the feet with tiny paring cuts that soften the angles. Blend each foot with its leg and each leg with the body using paring cuts on the legs.

11 **Release the figure.** Using V-cuts, shape the top of the frog as you work to separate the sculpture from the holding block. Fine-tune the top and back of the frog carving while paying close attention to symmetry. Using shallow V-cuts, establish small bumps for the eyes and blend it into the nose and back with paring cuts. Use paring strokes to establish a symmetrical mouth edge. On the entire carving, smooth any sharp edges and clean up any messy bits with paring cuts. Finally, drill a 1/16" (1.6mm) hole in the bottom of the figure and insert a toothpick to hold while painting.

12 **Paint the base color.** Mix blue paint with a little white and a touch of yellow to create a solidly dark blue color. Apply two coats of this blue on the legs and bottom and one coat on the head and back. Depending on the hue of your blue, adjust the amount of white and yellow in the mix to achieve the desired color.

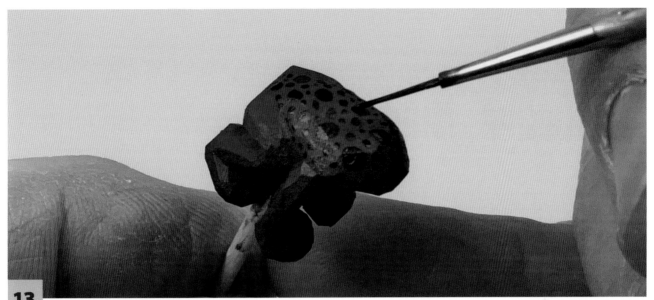

13 **Add features and details.** Use black paint for the eyes and spots. Pencil in the eyes before you begin to ensure symmetry. Using a circular motion, paint on the eyes. Make imperfectly round dots slightly smaller than the eyes randomly on the rest of the back. Fill in between these dots with smaller dots until the entire space of the back and head is filled with a dotted pattern.

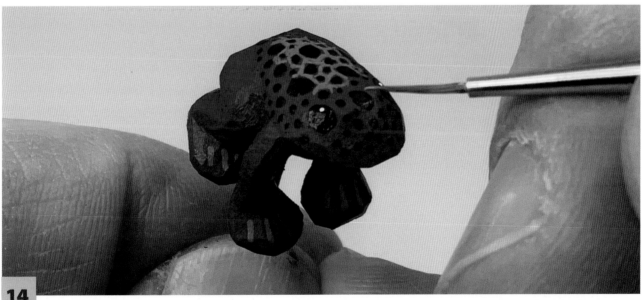

14 **Finish painting.** Mix the blue paint with about one-quarter as much white. Use this paint mix to outline the dots and eyes and paint toes on the feet. Add blue to the mix and use this color to outline the edges of the field of dots. Also use this color to make tiny dots on the rest of the dark blue field, including the legs and belly. Apply these dots randomly and sparingly. Finally, use white paint to make reflection dots in the eyes.

Patterns

Design: Minotaur

One hundred years ago and just fifty miles away from me in Weimar, Germany, the Bauhaus, a School of Art, emerged to leave an indelible mark on the modern world. The school pursued invention, playfulness, and clarity of design with a fervor guided by intuition and purpose that's still evidenced in the products of companies like Apple and IKEA. I've tried to use the essence of this philosophy in my work and, in particular, in the planning of this piece. The Minotaur was a beast of myth in the origin story of the Greek world, a murderous character confined inside a labyrinth. I've reinterpreted it as a toylike figure wrapped in a coat of chaotic confetti. The design is goofy, vibrant, and full of life-giving energy. In a spirit of levity, it's meant not to scare, but to delight; after all, small as it is, there's little chance of it being a bully—it could hardly hurt a flea.

Materials & Tools

- Wood: 1¾" tall x 1⅝" wide x ¾" thick (4.5 x 4.1 x 1.9cm), grain running vertically
- 1 toothpick
- Carving knife
- Hand protection
- Pin vise with ¹⁄₁₆" (1.6mm) drill bit
- Sandpaper: 200–400 grit and 600–800 grit
- Paintbrushes: #1 or larger round paintbrush, #10/0 liner or smaller detail brush
- Paints: red, blue, yellow, white, and black

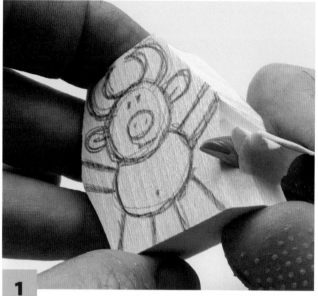

1 **Rough out.** Transfer the pattern to both sides of the wood. Use paring or push cuts to remove the material from the four corners of the block outside the boundaries of the pattern. You could rough out with a saw, but at this scale it doesn't take long to rough out with a knife.

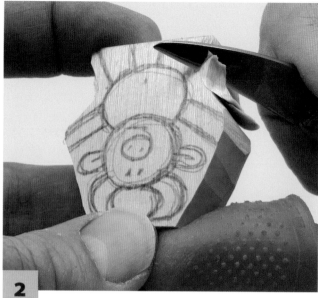

2 **Separate the limbs.** Use V-cuts to remove the material between the legs and arms. Once the excavated groove reaches the boundary with the body, use stop cuts to give definition to the transitions between the arm, body, and leg on each side. First, slice flush with the boundary of the leg or arm, then meet those cuts with knife strokes running flush with the body.

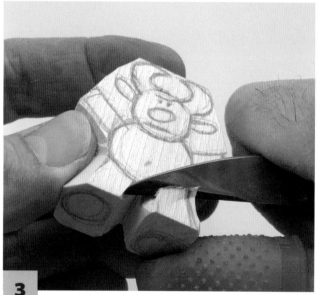

3 **Establish the legs.** Draw round footprints on the bottom of the wood, one near the front and the other near the back of the figure. Use V-cuts to establish separation between the left and right legs until the groove reaches the body region. Use paring or push cuts to shape the legs so that they leave the body at an angle to meet the footprints. Keep the thickness of the legs consistent from top to bottom.

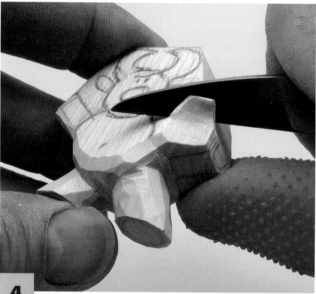

4 **Narrow the arms.** Draw the arms on the wood from three angles so that they appear to reach forward at an angle. Use paring and push cuts to narrow the arms; where they attach to the body, use stop cuts so that the thickness of the arms is consistent from the base to the tip. Make the first knife strokes flush along the length of the arm from the tip to the base and meet those cuts with knife strokes at the base, flush with the body.

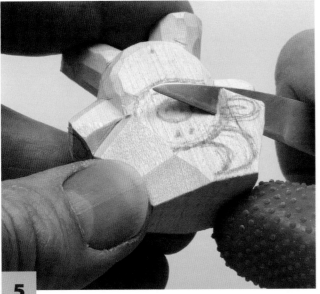

5 **Start work on the top of the head.** Use paring or push cuts to narrow the parts of the head region containing the horns and ears. Narrow the whole area both front and back until you've removed almost ¼" (6.4mm) from each side.

6 **Establish the boundary between the head and body.** Use V-cuts to make a groove between the head and body. Start by making an angled incision, a curved line that forms the boundary between head and body, and meet that cut with knife strokes that chip out the material, creating a groove. Expand the groove with repeated V-cuts. Use paring and push cuts to blend the groove with both the head and body.

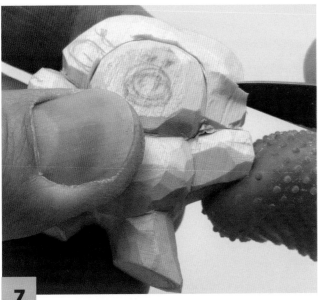

7 **Establish the boundary between the head and the horns and ears.** Using stop cuts, starting with an incision running flush with the curved boundary of the head and meet this cut with knife strokes that slice in from the ears and horns. Repeat on the backside of the head.

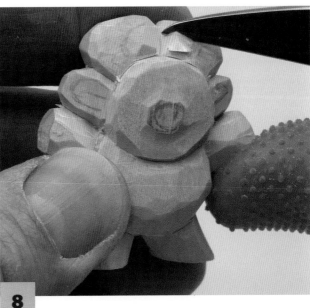

8 **Separate the left and right horns.** Use combination cuts to establish the gap between the horns. Start with V-cuts at the midpoint between the horns, then expand the groove with knife strokes that follow the inside curve of the horns, from the horn tip to the base. Next, chip out the wood with knife strokes that slice flush with the top of the head and meet the first set of cuts.

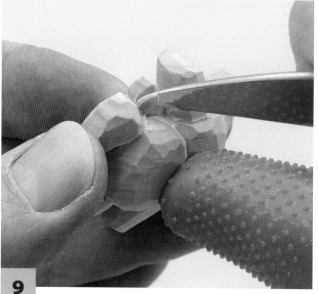

9 **Narrow and define the ears.** Use stop cuts to narrow the ears further. Start with knife strokes at the front and back of the ear and meet those cuts with knife strokes that slice flush with the surface of the head. On the top and bottom of each ear, start paring knife strokes at each of the tips and follow the curve of the ear to its base.

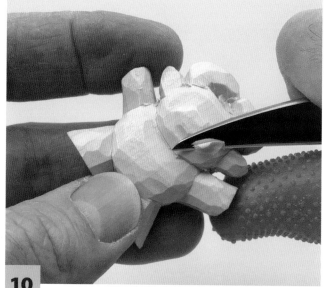

10 **Establish the nose.** Use paring or push cuts to shape the nose. Make knife strokes around the entire circumference of the nose using a scooping motion. Refine the ears and horns. Use paring and push cuts to fine-tune the ears and horns. Look at the figure from multiple angles; compare the left and right horn and the left and right ear to maintain symmetry. Take off just small amounts of material with each knife stroke.

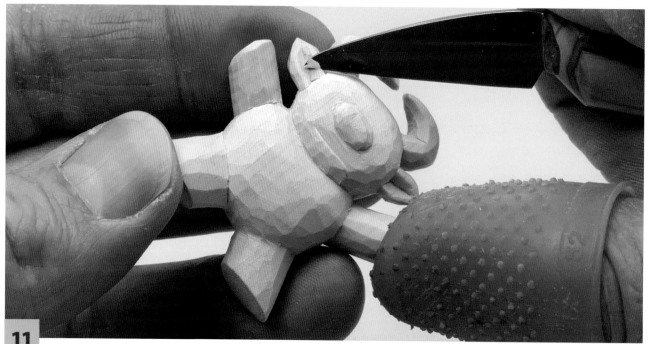

11 **Work on the ears and mouth.** Create a V-shaped groove to represent the mouth. Use the tip of the blade to make the first incision, and meet that cut with another knife stroke that runs the length of the first cut but at an angle of 90 degrees to the first. Next, use the blade tip to make a V-shaped groove in the ears. Start the knife strokes near the tip of each ear and slice toward the head, each angled so the cuts meet each other. Chip out the wood with a shallow cut at the base, flush with the head. Finally, drill a ¹⁄₁₆" (1.6mm) hole in the bottom of the figure and insert a toothpick to hold while painting.

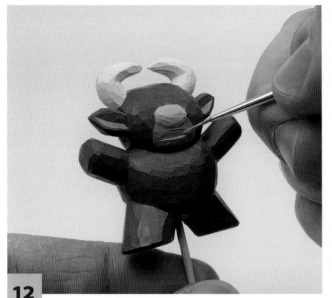

12 **Paint base colors.** Mix blue and a touch of white to create a blue color. Paint two coats on the head, body, arms, and legs. Mix a little white with the blue mixture to make a lighter blue. Apply the paint to the region below the nose and inside the ears. Mix white with a touch of black and yellow to create a cream color; apply this to the horns. Mix white with small amounts of yellow, red, and blue to create a tan color; apply this to the nose.

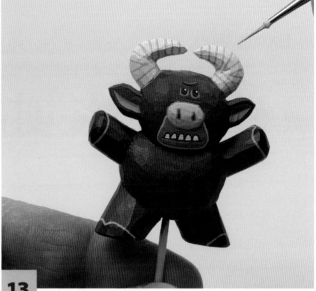

13 **Add features and details.** Use black to paint the eyes, eyebrow, nostrils, hooves, and mouth. Mix red, blue, yellow, and white to create a light brown and outline the nostrils with this color. Use white to paint the teeth and the reflections in the eyes. Use black to outline the teeth. Mix blue with white to create a light blue color, and outline the hooves, muzzle, and half the eyes. Mix white with a touch of red, yellow, and blue to create a gray color to paint lines on the horns.

Pattern

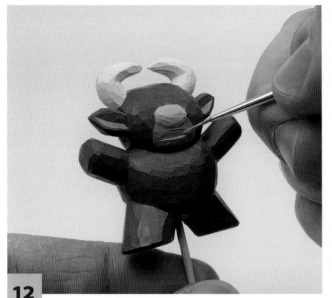

14 **Add fur texture.** Mix red, blue, yellow, and white to create a brown color to paint hash marks randomly over the entire body. Add more white to the mix to create a tan color, then add more hash marks to the figure. Add more white to create a cream color, and repeat. Add yellow to the mix to create a golden color and add golden dots between the hash marks. Add red to the mix to create an orange color and add a few more dots. The effect should be one of chaos, like falling confetti or an explosion of color.

Nature: Sea Turtle

Snorkeling with sea turtles is like time travel: these ancient creatures fly through the water on flippers, and they've done so swimmingly since flowers first bloomed. Amongst coral and kelp teaming with life, the world engages our senses and forces us to consider the spectacle. The more we look at nature, the more beauty she reveals: the order, the forms, the details, the colors, the characters, the seasons. Nature is creation eternally refreshed, and without her, we no longer exist. The story that says earth rides on the back of a giant sea turtle, that we're all in the same boat, expresses this sentiment in the simplest possible terms. This carving is an homage to the natural world, the source of the substance and subject of my work. It's largely a naturalistic treatment, a mirror to the minutiae of nature, designed to pleasure the eye. As with all my work, I've used some artistic freedom by exaggerating the features, thereby giving the figure a somewhat caricatured look.

Materials & Tools

- Wood: ⅜" thick x 2¼" wide x 1⅝" long (1 x 5.7 x 4.1cm), grain running from head to tail (long dimension)
- 1 toothpick
- Carving knife
- Hand protection

- Pin vise with 1/16" (1.6mm) drill bit
- Sandpaper: 200–400 grit and 600–800 grit
- Paintbrushes: #1 or larger round paintbrush, #10/0 liner or smaller detail brush
- Paints: red, blue, yellow, white, and black to mix shades of orange and creamy white

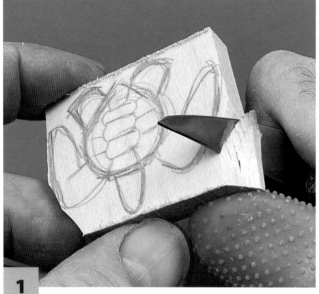

1 **Rough out.** Transfer the pattern to both sides of the wood. Use paring or push cuts to round the four corners. Don't carve all the way to the guideline—leave a little extra material to remove later. Use paring or push cuts to thin the flippers so they slope to about half the original thickness at the edges.

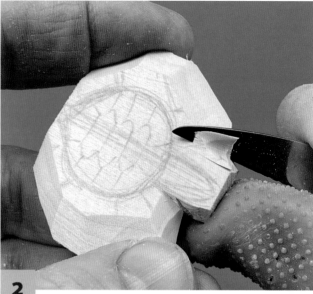

2 **Establish the head.** Use stop cuts to remove the material from between the head and the front two flippers. Make the first knife stroke parallel to the side of the head and meet that cut with a diagonal stroke from the direction of the flipper. Continue to deepen the groove until it reaches the front of the shell.

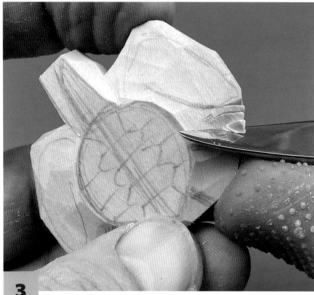

3 **Separate the flippers.** Use stop cuts to separate the front from the rear flippers. Make the first knife strokes at the tip of the front flipper and match those cuts with knife strokes starting at the front side of the rear flipper to chip out the material. Extend the groove forward to remove material between the front flipper and the shell with a series of V-cuts.

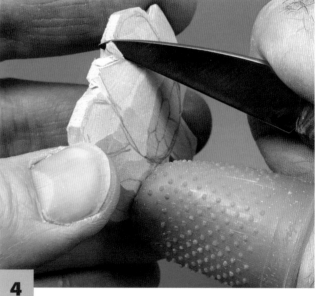

4 **Define the rear flippers.** Use stop cuts to remove the material between the rear flippers and the tail section of the shell. Make the first knife strokes at the border of the shell and meet those cuts with knife strokes between the rear flippers to chip out the wood. Expand the groove with repeated V-cuts until it reaches the shell.

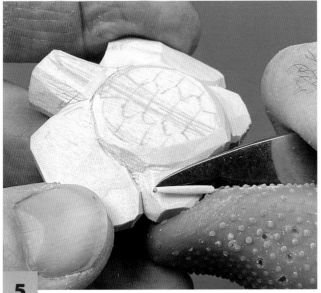

5 **Thin the rear flippers.** Use paring or push cuts to thin the rear flippers so they slope to the edges. Trim to about one-quarter of their original thickness. Redraw the rear flippers on the wood and use paring or push cuts to shape the rear flippers. Be aware of the direction of the grain so that you don't accidentally chip out the wood and ruin a flipper.

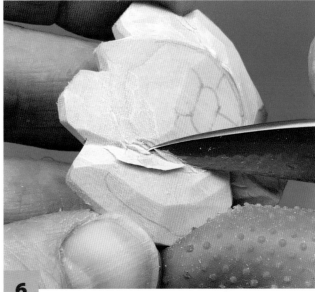

6 **Define the front flippers.** Use V-cuts to further excavate the groove between the front flippers and the shell. Make the V-cuts on both the top and bottom of the figure; continue to deepen the grooves until they meet and a gap is formed. Redraw the front flippers on the wood and use paring or push cuts to shape the flippers toward their final form. Pay attention to the grain direction: the outside of the flipper should be carved from back to front, and the inside, the opposite.

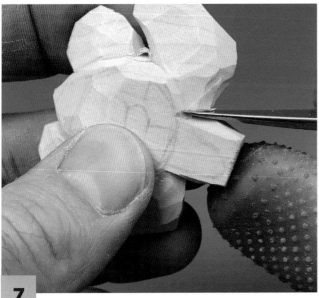

7 **Refine the front end of the figure.** Use stop cuts to narrow the head and expand the distance between the neck and the base of the front flippers. Begin the first knife stroke at the head and cut in the direction of the shell. Match this cut with knife strokes from the base of the flipper toward the neck. Use paring cuts beginning at the base of the neck and proceeding toward the flippers to expand the distance between the two features.

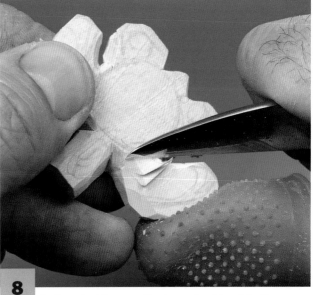

8 **Define the flippers.** On the underside of the figure, use V-cuts to make grooves at the base of all the flippers. Make the first knife strokes flush with the curved belly of the turtle and match these cuts with knife strokes that slice across the width of the flipper where it connects to the body. Be careful not to cut too deeply—leave the flippers thick enough at the base to retain strength, about ⅛" (3.2mm).

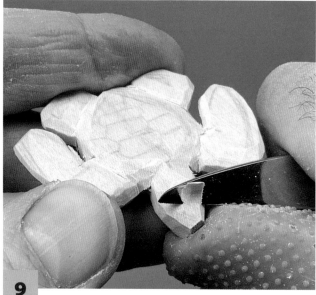

9 **Define the head.** Using paring or push cuts, narrow the neck and head to the final dimensions. Taper the nose portion from underneath so that the head is pointing slightly upward. Mark the eyes and mouth with a pencil and look at the head from various angles. Correct for symmetry and any other flaws you may find.

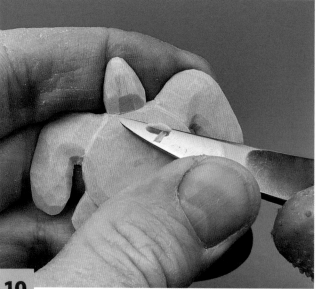

10 **Define the shell.** Using paring or push cuts, smooth the curve of the shell, paying special attention to symmetry. On the belly, use paring or push cuts to blend the bottom of the figure with the transitions to the flippers and head. Draw the shell on the wood with pencil, including the borders for each scute (plate), to test for symmetry. Trim the outside edge of the shell with paring cuts to smooth the curve.

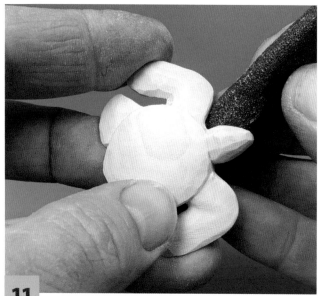

11 **Sand.** Start with a coarse (200–400-grit) sandpaper to smooth the entire surface of the figure. Be careful not to remove too much material. When the figure looks smooth, switch to a finer (600–800-grit) sandpaper to bring the surface to an even smoother finish. I like a smooth surface for detailed painting, but it is not essential. Feel free to leave the figure raw and spend more time cleaning up any messy areas. Finally, drill a ⅟₁₆" (1.6mm) hole in the bottom of the figure and insert a toothpick to hold while painting.

12 **Paint the base colors.** Draw the eyes, mouth, and shell pattern on the wood. Mix yellow with white to create a light yellow: paint the eyes with two coats. While the paint is still wet, mix the yellow with more white and blend this color at the top of the eyes. Use black to paint the mouth, pupil, eye outlines, and the shell pattern. Use white to make the reflection dot in each pupil. Mix white with yellow and a touch of red and blue to create a light golden color and apply two coats over the entire body outside the black lines.

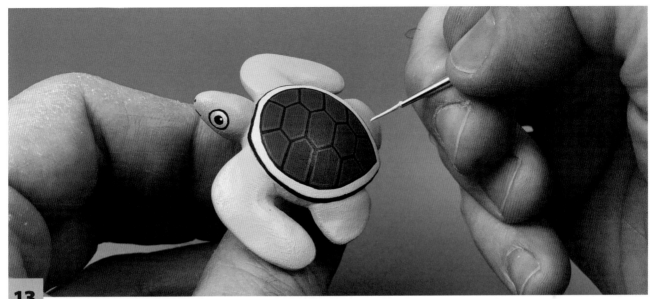

13 **Work on the shell.** Mix red with yellow and a touch of blue and white to create a brownish red color. Apply two coats of this color to each of the shell scutes (plates). Add yellow to the mix and outline the scutes with this color. Repaint the black shell lines with black paint. Mix white with a touch of black and yellow to get an off-white hue, then apply this color to the ring around the shell.

Pattern

14 **Add texture.** Mix red with yellow and small amounts of blue, black, and white to create a dark orange color, then paint irregular, round dots on the head, flippers, and along the sides of the body. Pay special attention to the larger dots on the head and flippers. Mix the dark orange with yellow; paint smaller dots in the middle of the first set of dots. Mix white with a touch of black and yellow to create an off-white to paint a web of imprecise lines between all the dots.

Sculpture: Kiwi

Sometimes I call myself a whittler because it accurately describes my method and has a folksy, accessible feel to it. But my carvings are also sculpture, a word that signals the serious work that goes into the design of each piece and makes it "art." Since "art" is now used to describe every skilled act, "sculpture" is the more useful term. Sculpture is not a homogenous field; it includes everything from totem poles to Michelangelo. My carvings are often more figurative than literal—I'm not trying to carve the thing exactly as it is, but rather in a close approximation that intends to capture the essence of the creature. Sometimes the subject matter speaks to me. For example, this Kiwi, a flightless bird without the ability to soar, questions what freedoms are sacrificed for comfort. The design's round head and body and the linear beak and legs play off each other; the composition breaks with realism to proffer an abstract perspective on the bird at hand.

Materials & Tools

- Wood: ¾" x 1³⁄₁₆" x 1½" (1.9 x 3 x 3.8cm), grain running in the longest dimension
- 1 toothpick
- Carving knife
- Hand protection
- Pin vise with ¹⁄₁₆" (1.6mm) drill bit
- Sandpaper: 200–400 grit and 600–800 grit
- Paintbrushes: #1 or larger round paintbrush, #10/0 liner or smaller detail brush
- Paints: red, blue, yellow, white, and black to mix shades of brown and gold

1 **Rough out.** Transfer the pattern to the wood. Use paring and push cuts to round all four edges of the top and sides. Draw two circles on the top for the head and body and two footprints on the bottom for the feet to help you determine how much material you can safely remove.

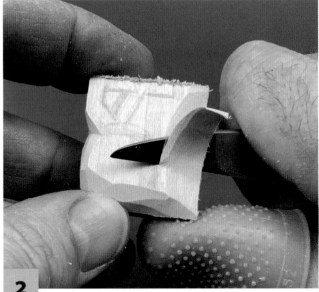

2 **Narrow the head and beak.** Use paring or push cuts. Redraw the circle for the head on the top of the wood and use it as a guide. Make sure you have drawn the footprints on the bottom of the wood—use these markings to make sure you don't cut off a toe on the most forward foot.

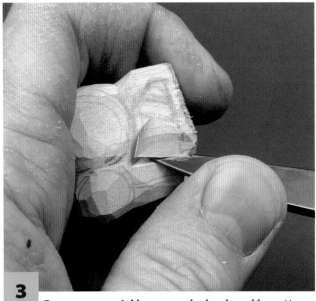

3 **Remove material between the beak and legs.** Use three-stroke combination cuts with cuts along the front of the belly, the front side of the legs, and the backside of the beak. It doesn't matter in what order you make these cuts, but pay attention to the grain of the wood, and leave a little extra material on all sides to remove later.

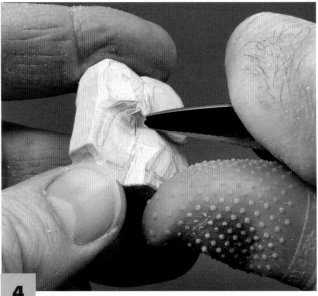

4 **Keep working between the beak and legs.** Continue excavating at the same location with combination cuts until you hollow the space. Use three- and four-stroke combination cuts with cuts on the front of the belly and legs, the backside of the beak, and the top of the feet. Redraw the figure from the side to help keep track of how much material you need to remove. Be careful cutting across the grain on the feet; angle your cuts slightly so that you put less pressure on the foot.

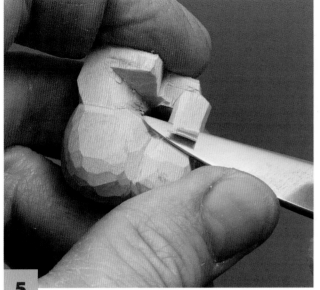

5 **Narrow the beak.** Start with push or paring cuts. Use stop cuts where the beak and foot nearly meet. Make the first knife stroke flush with the top of the foot and follow that with a matching cut from the head, proceeding down the length of the beak. Keep the beak attached to the front foot and use controlled cuts to make sure you don't slice through the foot.

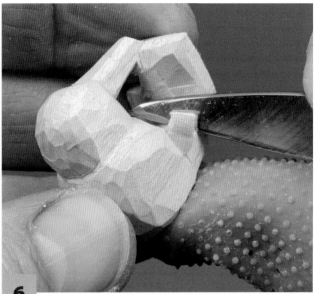

6 **Define the legs and feet.** Using stop cuts, push cuts, and paring cuts, narrow the legs and establish the borders between the body, legs, and feet. Use stop cuts at the junction of the body and legs with the first knife stroke running along the curve of the body and the secondary strokes coming from the legs to meet the first cut. Use stop cuts at the feet as well, with the first cut flush with the top of the foot and the secondary cuts on the legs.

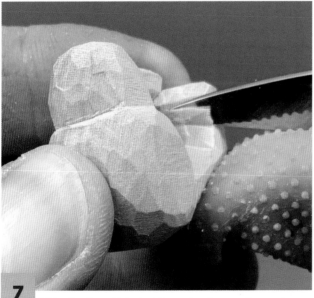

7 **Thin the feet.** Using paring or push cuts, shave a layer of wood off the top of the feet. Start the knife strokes at the front and sides of the foot and push or pull the knife carefully toward the leg. You'll be cutting across the grain over a thin piece of wood, so try not to put too much pressure on the feet by only taking off small amounts at a time. Use paring cuts to define the outside of the footprint.

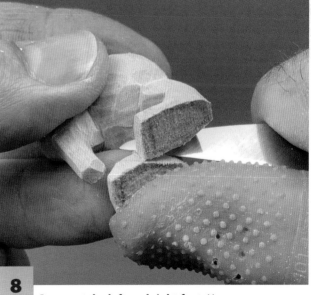

8 **Separate the left and right feet.** Use stop cuts to excavate between the legs from the back. Make the first knife strokes flush with the curve of the belly and match those cuts with strokes from the legs to the belly. Use paring cuts to chip out the material between the feet. Once you've reached separation, round the edges of the feet.

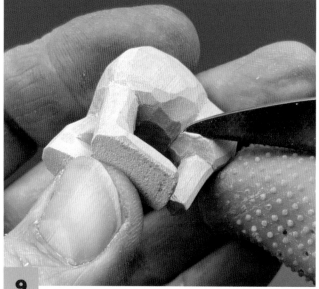

9 **Define the head.** Using V-cuts, define the transition from the head to the body. Use paring or push cuts to smooth the transition and establish the curves of the head. Look at the head from all angles to check for symmetry. Clean up any fuzzy spots, smooth any sharp edges, and round the head. Make final refinements to the beak and the border with the head using stop and paring cuts.

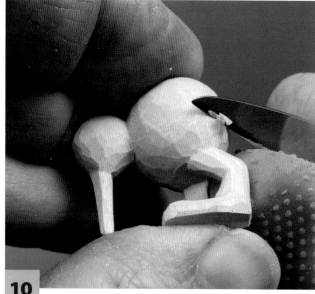

10 **Define the body and legs.** Look over the entire figure, watching for asymmetric, sharp, or misshapen areas. Use push or paring cuts to smooth the curves and establish a rounded appearance. Clean up the junction with the legs using paring or push cuts. Make sure both legs and feet are about the same size. Make sure the whole figure looks pleasingly proportionate.

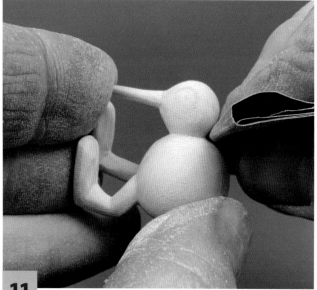

11 **Sand.** Using a coarse (200–400-grit) sandpaper, lightly sand the entire figure, giving special attention to the roundness of the body and head. Be careful not to put too much pressure on delicate parts like the feet. Switch to a finer (600–800-grit) sandpaper to make the finish even smoother. To sand the top of the feet, place the figure on a table while you sand to avoid breakage. Finally, drill a ¹⁄₁₆" (1.6mm) hole in the bottom of the figure and insert a toothpick to hold while painting.

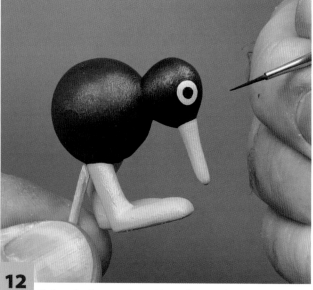

12 **Paint the base colors.** Mix yellow with a touch of red, blue, and white to create a golden color to apply to the legs, feet, and beak. Draw the eyes on the wood. Mix yellow and a touch of white paint to create a light yellow; apply this color to the eye. Lighten the yellow further and apply this color to the top of the eye, then blend. Use black to paint the pupil and a circle around the eye. Mix black, red, and yellow to create a dark brown and apply two coats of this to the entire unpainted portion of the figure.

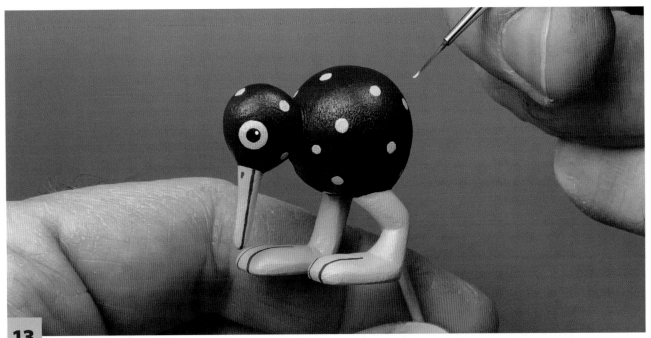

13 **Start patterning.** Mix yellow with red and blue to get a brown color; paint details on the feet, legs, and beak. Mix yellow and white to create a light yellow color; make dots randomly around the entire brown color field. Use white paint to add a small reflection dot in each eye.

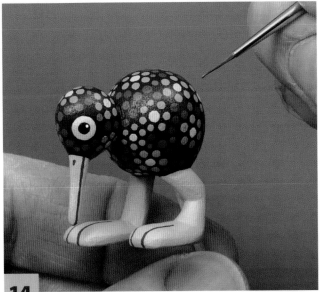

14 **Finish patterning.** Mix yellow, white, and red to get a light orange. Make rings of orange dots around each yellow dot from the previous step. Mix red, yellow, and black to create a dark red color. Make red dots next to the orange dots. Mix yellow and white with the dark red mix to get a brown color. Add brown dots to the remaining blank areas of the dark brown color field.

Pattern

Painting: Rooster

Barnyard life is often short and brutish for the average rooster. Around half of eggs hatch male, but you only need one cockerel for every dozen or so hens, so the math is not in their favor. What they miss in longevity, though, they make up for in finery, their feathers as fiery as a phoenix. When painting such a detailed and colorful animal, I usually simplify patterns but keep the colors as true as possible. I start by painting all of the base colors. When I start on the details, I pay close attention to the effect of light on the actual creature's coat; the shimmer of iridescence can be simulated with points of lighter color. A dense mix of hues can be abstracted by selecting a few prominent colors for the pattern. Building knowledge with each new project develops the painting vocabulary that allows one to more successfully express through color and represent reality in a condensed form.

Materials & Tools

- Wood: ⅝" x 1" x 2⅛" (1.6 x 2.5 x 5.4cm), grain running in the longest dimension
- Several toothpicks
- Dowel or branch: ⅝" (1.6cm) dia. or larger, piece cut to ³⁄₁₆" (4.8mm) long/thick
- Carving knife
- Hand protection
- Pin vise with ¹⁄₁₆" (1.6mm) drill bit
- Sandpaper: 200–400 grit and 600–800 grit
- Paintbrushes: #1 or larger round paintbrush, #10/0 liner or smaller detail brush
- Paints: red, blue, yellow, white, and black to mix a large variety of colors

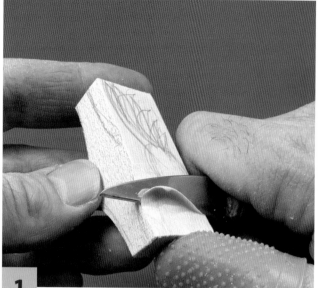

1 **Narrow the wood.** Before applying the pattern, use paring or push cuts to narrow the sides of the ends of a piece of wood. Narrow one end starting about ½" (1.3cm) from the end; this will be the head end. For the tail, narrow the wood starting about 1" (2.5cm) from the end. Narrow equally on both sides of each end so that the remaining material is about ¼" (6.4mm) wide.

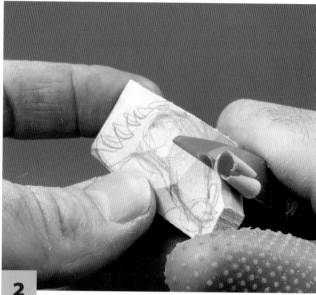

2 **Rough out.** Transfer the pattern to both sides of the wood. Remove the material below the head in front of the body using push or paring cuts. Be careful not to remove material to be used later to fashion the wattles, those red bits of flesh that hang down under the beak.

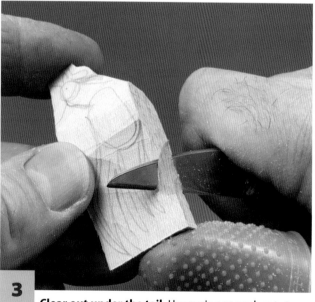

3 **Clear out under the tail.** Use paring or push cuts to remove the material from under and behind the tail section. Round the edges of the body section and blend it to the cuts you've made for both the head and tail sections.

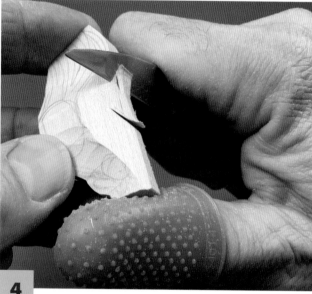

4 **Clear out the top.** Use V-cuts to remove the material between the head and tail above the back. Create the arc of the tail. Use stop cuts at the tip of the comb to remove the material behind the head. Start with knife strokes at the comb's tip, slicing in the direction of the body, and meet those cuts with knife strokes starting from the base of the tail.

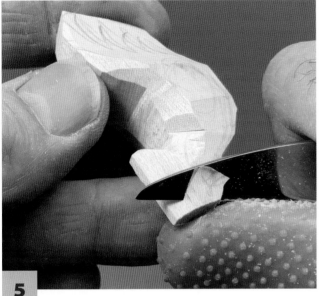

5 **Narrow the head, comb, and beak using push cuts.**
Narrow the beak to a point at its tip and the top of the comb to about ⅛" (3.2mm). Redraw the head and comb on both sides of the wood and use stop cuts to define the comb. Start the first knife stroke at the top of the comb, slicing carefully downward toward the head, and meet that cut with a knife stroke that's flush with the top of the head.

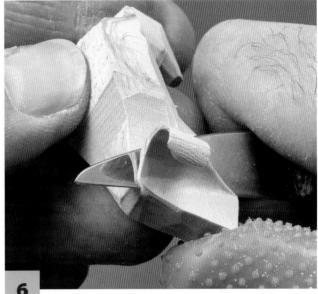

6 **Separate the back of the neck and comb.** Use stop cuts to establish this separation. Use paring or push cuts to narrow the tail, blend the back of the neck with the body, and round the edges of the body to blend it front and back.

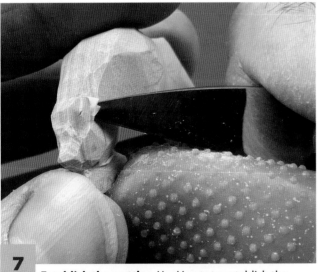

7 **Establish the wattles.** Use V-cuts to establish the boundary between the beak, neck, and wattle. Start with a curved, shallow knife stroke slicing flush with the front of the neck. Begin the cut at the end of the wattle area and slice toward the beak. Meet this cut with a second knife stroke slicing flush with the outside of the wattle. Make a three-stroke combination cut to separate the wattle area into two wattles. First, make two cuts in the middle of the wattle area to form an upside-down V. For the third cut, jab the tip of the knife into the wood, flush with the front of the neck, to chip out the piece.

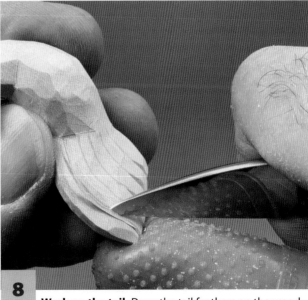

8 **Work on the tail.** Draw the tail feathers on the wood, making sure that the lines meet at the tips of the feathers. Start with small V-cuts at these tips, then, using the tip of the knife, make pairs of long incisions along the length of each of the lines you've drawn to establish a groove between each feather. To avoid messy splinters, try to make each groove with just a single pair of knife strokes.

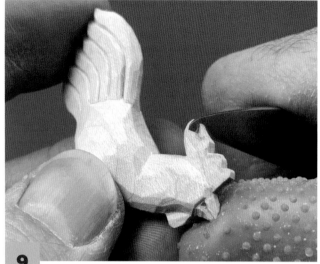

9 **Work on the beak and comb.** Using the tip of the knife blade, make a pair of shallow incisions on each side of the beak to separate the top from the bottom. Start the cuts at the base of the beak and slice toward the tip. Next, make shallow, controlled V-cuts to establish the points of the comb. Start with knife strokes at the front of the comb and meet the cut from further into the middle. Likewise with the back of the comb, start at the furthest point and slice in toward the middle first. This helps to avoid breaking off the ends of the comb where it is most fragile. Once the dips are complete, use paring or push cuts to further narrow the comb to its final thickness.

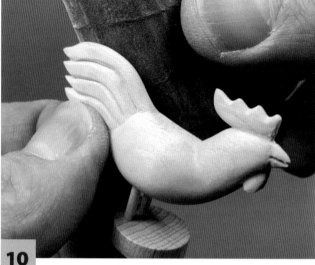

10 **Make the base and legs and sand.** Following steps 9 and 11 from the Duck project, create a base and two toothpick legs and drill holes in the rooster's body to receive the legs. Sand the rooster, first with a coarse (200–400-grit) sandpaper and then with a finer (600–800-grit) sandpaper, but don't use the coarse sandpaper on the most delicate parts. Glue the legs into the base and the body. Finally, drill a 1⁄16" (1.6mm) hole in the bottom of the figure and insert a toothpick to hold while painting.

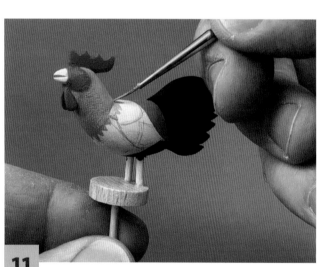

11 **Paint the base colors.** Mix red, yellow, and white paint to create a pink color. Apply two coats to the comb, face, and wattle. Mix yellow with white and red paint to create a light orange color; paint the neck or cape this color. Use a detail brush to finish the detailed areas of the cape. Add more yellow to the mix to vary the color within the field, especially where it meets the body area with a jagged line. Mix a slightly darker orange and paint the saddle or back of the rooster. Use black paint for the tail and rump.

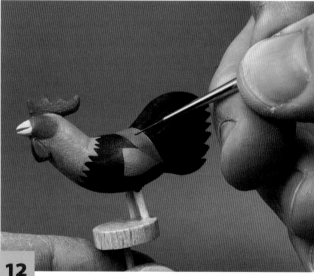

12 **Paint the rest of the body.** Mix red, black, and small amounts of black and blue paint to create a dark red color; apply this to the back. Mix black with blue and a touch of white to create a dark blue color; apply this to the breast. Mix yellow with small amounts of red, white, and a touch of blue to create a golden color; apply this to the wing areas. Mix blue with a little black and yellow to create a blue color; apply this to the triangular areas above the wings.

13 **Start painting details.** Mix black and white and a touch of yellow to create a gray color to paint the legs, feet, and beak. Add more white to the mix and add short hash marks to the legs and feet and the top of the beak. Add even more white to paint the nails. Mix yellow, blue, and white to create a green color for between the feet. Use white to paint the ears and black for the eyes, and add a white spot on each eye for a reflection. Mix blue with small amounts of yellow, white, and black to create a blue color to paint a pattern of short, thick hash marks on the breast. Add black and yellow to the mix to get a dark green color and paint a line in each of the tail grooves.

14 **Finish the head and neck.** Use a detail brush and yellow paint to outline three-quarters of each eye, then mix red and a little black to create a dark red color to outline each eye. Mix red, yellow, and a touch of blue to create a dark orange color. Use a detail brush to paint lines from the face to halfway down the neck. Paint yellow lines in the opposite direction starting at the jagged end of the cape.

15 **Finish the body.** Mix red, white, and black to create a grayish red color. Paint lines in the dark red area. Add white to the mix and make a dozen random dots there too. Mix red, yellow, and blue to create orange, then paint faint lines on the orange wings and wavy lines in the orange saddle. Use yellow paint to make hash marks on the saddle. Add five black dots to the wings and outline those dots halfway with a yellow and white mixture. Mix blue and white, then paint faint hash marks in the blue triangles. Add more white and make faint hash marks in the triangles, on the breast, and on the tail feathers.

Pattern

Caricature: Dog

The variety of dog breeds is a testament to the malleability of nature's building blocks. Who would have thought that within the genetic lair of the wolf hid a teacup Shih Tzu? Dogs are caricatures in the flesh: the selective breeding of dogs by humans for specific jobs like hunting, guarding, or cuddling has unnaturally chosen certain traits and exaggerated them. Caricature is an effective way to stretch your drawing skills, and turning caricatures into carvings will give you feedback on the limits of carving and teach you how to go about planning projects going forward. The variety and ubiquity of dogs in human culture means artists have a lot of material to choose from. I like to choose just one trait to exaggerate, so, for this design, I chose the nose, drawing attention to this dubious canine superpower. After all, if a dog's sense of smell is so good, why don't they sniff flowers rather than rear ends and dead toads?

Materials & Tools

- Wood: ¾" thick x 1" tall x 1¾" long (1.9 x 2.5 x 4.5cm), grain running vertically
- 1 toothpick
- Carving knife
- Detail knife (optional)
- Hand protection

- Pin vise with ¹⁄₁₆" (1.6mm) drill bit
- Paintbrushes: #1 or larger round paintbrush, #10/0 liner or smaller detail brush
- Paints: red, blue, yellow, white, and black to mix shades of brown

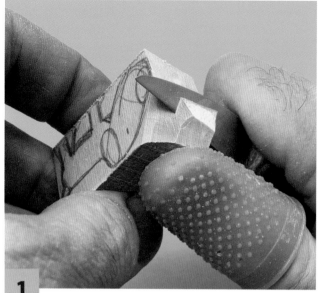

1

Rough out. Transfer the pattern to the wood. Use paring or push cuts to remove the material from above and in front of the head. The knife strokes will be nearly across the grain, so take it slow, work the edges, and use a repetitive method rather than trying to remove all the material at once.

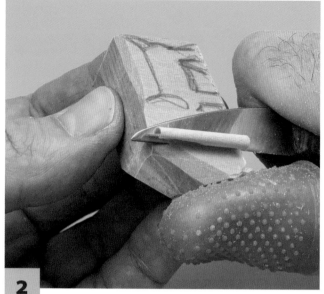

2

Narrow the head. Use paring or push cuts to narrow the head about 1⁄16" (1.6mm) on each side and round the edges between the top and sides of the head. Start the knife strokes in front of the ears and direct the cuts toward the muzzle. Be careful not to remove too much material.

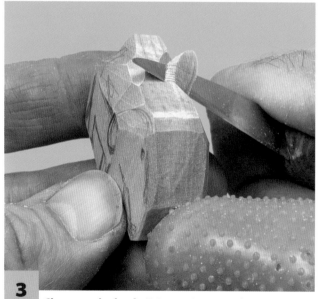

3

Clear out the back. Using paring or push cuts, remove the material above the back between the tail and head. Repeat these cuts until you've excavated nearly all the way to the guidelines of the head, back, and tail. The knife strokes will be nearly across the grain, so take it slow. Use paring or push cuts again to narrow the tail section to about half the thickness of the wood.

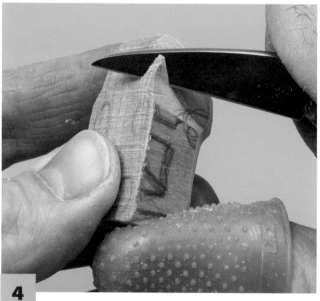

4

Work on the chest. Pencil in footprints on the bottom of the wood. Use V-cuts to remove the material from under the head and in front of the front legs. Make the first knife strokes at the front of the legs and match those cuts with knife strokes that start at the chin and meet the first set of cuts. These second sets of cuts will be across the grain; take off only small bits of material with each stroke.

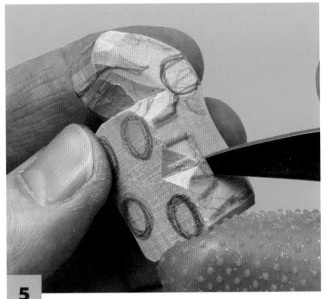

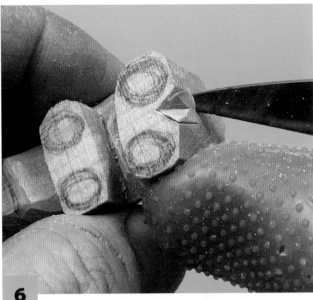

5 **Separate the front legs from the back legs.** Use V-cuts between the front and back legs, using the footprints you drew as a guide. Make combination cuts in the same location, with the first two knife strokes on the insides of the legs and the third stroke flush with the belly. Continue with a mix of V-cuts and combination cuts to clear out the material.

6 **Separate the left and right back legs.** Use V-cuts to remove the material. Once the groove has reached the border of the belly, switch to stop cuts, with the first knife strokes following the edge of the legs. Make the matching strokes flush with the belly, between the legs, to chip out the wood. You may want to use a detail knife, as it's a tight space.

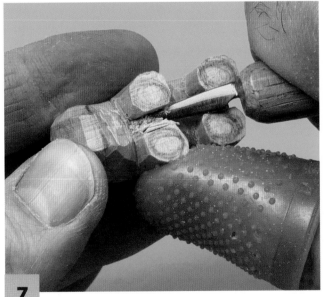

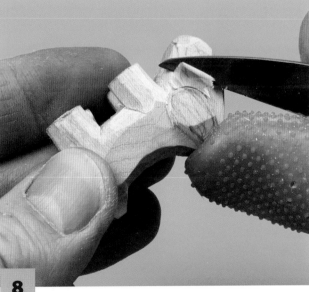

7 **Separate the left and right front legs.** Follow the instructions in the previous step to separate the left and right front legs.

8 **Establish the ears.** Redraw the ears on the wood. Use paring or push cuts to remove material from outside the guidelines. At the tip of the ear, use stop cuts to establish the border. Make the first knife stroke into the wood at the guideline and follow that with a stroke from below that meets the first cut and chips out the material. Proceed around the front and back of the ear as well, using stop cuts in a similar manner.

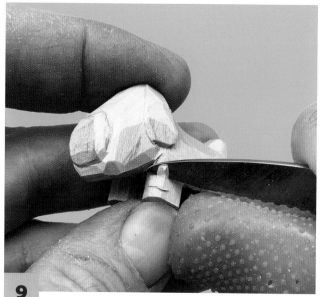

9 **Establish the nose and paws.** Use V-cuts on the sides of the muzzle to define the nose. Use paring cuts to define the front and back of the nose. Use stop cuts to establish the paws. Start with knife strokes on the topside of the paws and meet those cuts with knife strokes starting at the base of the leg, directed toward the first set of cuts.

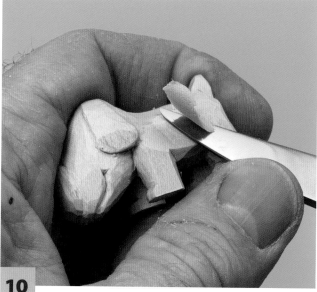

10 **Round the body.** Use paring or push cuts to trim the tail down to its final size. On the top of the tail, cut toward the body, but on the bottom, cut toward the tail's tip. At the base of the tail, use stop cuts to establish a clean transition. Use paring or push cuts to round the entire body and legs. Smooth the sharp edges and clean up any fuzzy areas on the belly or the base of the legs.

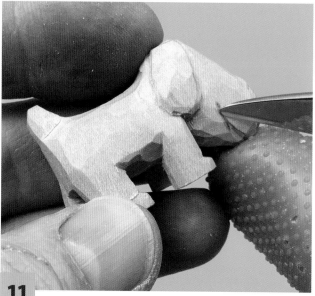

11 **Establish the mouth.** Draw the mouth on the wood. Make an incision with the tip of the knife along the entire length of the mouth, then match that cut with a second incision that draws along the same guideline but at an angle. Repeat to refine the mouth. Try to make long knife strokes so as not to leave a lot of leftover slivers hanging on in the groove. Finally, drill a ¹⁄₁₆" (1.6mm) hole in the bottom of the figure and insert a toothpick to hold while painting.

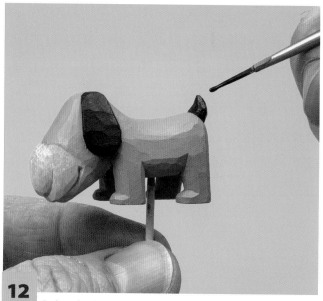

12 **Paint the base colors.** Mix red, yellow, blue, and black paint to create a dark reddish brown color; apply two coats to the tail and ears. Mix yellow with white and a touch of red and blue until you create a light golden color, then apply two coats of this mix to the head, body, and legs.

13 **Work on the nose and face.** Mark the eyes, nose, and mouth with a pencil, then use black to paint them. Use white paint on the muzzle and chin and make a reflection dot in each eye. Mix the reddish brown with white to create a brownish gray. Use this to make three short lines on each foot for toes. Mix the light golden color with white to get a lighter gold; outline the eyes and muzzle. Mix white with black to create a gray color; paint gray dots for the nostrils.

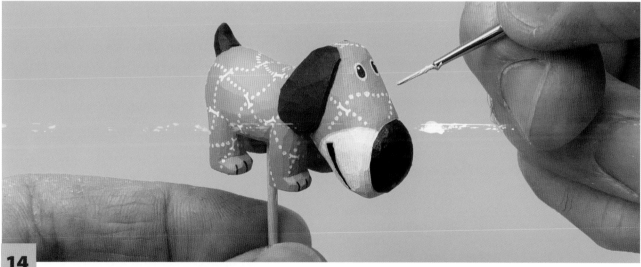

14 **Add patterning.** Mix blue and white for a light blue and paint tiny bones over the entire light golden area; for each bone, paint a line and add two dots on each end. Vary the angles of bones in relation to each other and keep distance between them. Mix white and yellow to create a very light yellow; paint trails of dots between the bones and to the edges of the golden color field.

Pattern

Aquarium Anglerfish

Boxes are symbolic of secrets, and this "matchbox aquarium's" dormant connection is to the classical elements of fire and water. It's also an exceptionally tiny space. The relationship between the size of the box and the size of the fish will determine the feel of the piece: spaciousness will suggest a more peaceful and natural environment, but if the fish dominates the space, it will take on a more cramped feeling, even comedic or cautionary. For this project, I've chosen a type of anglerfish, the triplewart seadevil, because I like strange fish even more when they have creepy names. Predators of the deep, dark ocean, all anglerfish carry with them a lure: a light on the end of a stem protruding from their forehead with which to attract fish to eat. Included in this project are several minnows to keep the beast fed.

Materials & Tools

grain running in the longest dimension for all pieces

- Wood (fish), 1 piece: ⅜" x ⅝" x 1⅛" (1 x 1.6 x 2.9cm)
- Wood (sandy seafloor), 1 piece: 3/32" thick x 1¾" x ⅝" (2.4mm x 4.5cm x 1.6cm)
- Wood (box back), 1 piece: 3/32" thick x 1¹⁵/₁₆" x 1¼" (2.4mm x 4.9cm x 3.2cm)
- Wood (box top and bottom), 2 pieces: 3/32" thick x 7/16" wide x 1¹⁵/₁₆" long (2.4mm x 1.1cm x 4.9cm)
- Wood (box sides), 2 pieces: 3/32" thick x 7/16" wide x 1¹/₁₆" long (2.4mm x 1.1cm x 2.7cm)
- Several toothpicks
- Carving knife
- Hand protection
- Pin vise with 1/16" (1.6mm) and 1/32" (0.8mm) drill bits
- Sandpaper: 600–800 grit
- Paintbrushes: #1 or larger round paintbrush, #10/0 liner or smaller detail brush
- Paints: red, blue, yellow, white, and black to mix a variety of colors
- 1" (2.5cm) piece of fishing line
- 1" (2.5cm) piece of 20-gauge shapeable wire
- Wire cutters/snips
- Wood glue
- Super glue
- Miniature table saw (optional) (to cut wood for the box)

Actual size

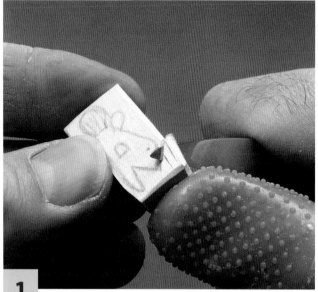

1 **Rough out the front end.** Transfer the fish pattern to the correct piece of wood. Use push or paring cuts to remove the material from under the body and chin from the base of the underside fin to the mouth. Use paring or push cuts to remove the material from above and in front of the head.

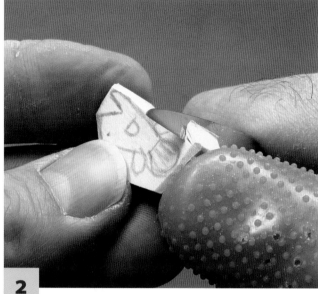

2 **Rough out the rear end.** Use paring or push cuts to remove material from under the tail. Leave material for the underside fin in place. Use paring or push cuts to remove the material behind the head above the dorsal fin and all the way to the tail. Leave the material for the dorsal fin in place.

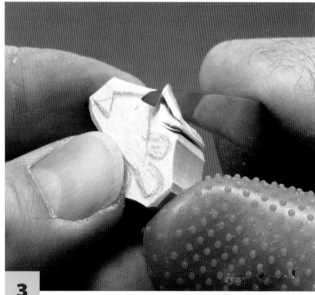

3 **Work along the top.** Use V-cuts to remove material from between the front of the dorsal fin and the hump of the head. Start with knife strokes at the highest point of the dorsal fin directed forward. Meet those cuts with knife strokes in the opposite direction starting at the highest point of the hump that forms the head.

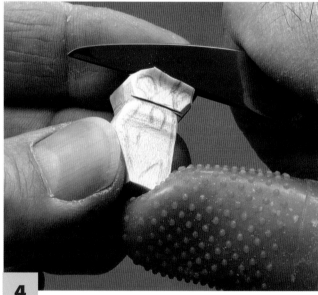

4 **Narrow the figure.** Use paring or push cuts to narrow the front of the figure. Start the knife strokes at the base of the pectoral fin and direct the cuts toward the mouth and nose. Narrow the tail with paring or push cuts, removing more material on the right side of the figure so that the tail will be slightly turned. Use stop cuts to narrow the rear end of the figure. Make the first knife strokes at the tips of the pectoral fins and meet those cuts with knife strokes starting at the tail.

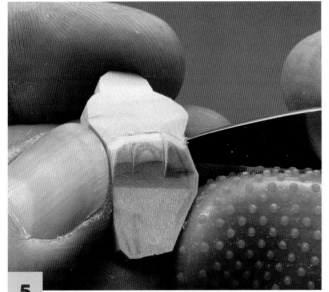

5   **Define the pectoral fins.** Use paring cuts to establish the angle at which the pectoral fins are connected to the body. Start the knife strokes at the tip of the fin and slice toward the base. Redraw the pectoral fins. Use stop cuts on the borders at the top and bottom of the pectoral fins. First, make shallow knife strokes on the border of the fin, then meet those cuts with cuts that run flush with the surface of the body to chip out the wood.

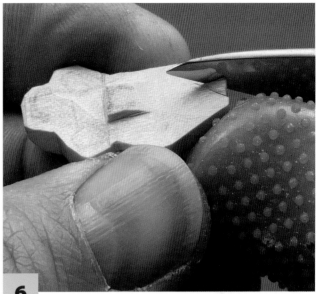

6   **Define the mouth.** Redraw the mouth, then use V-cuts to make a groove for it. Use the tip of the knife on the side of the figure, following the guidelines you just drew. Make the first cut along the inside of the lower jaw and meet that cut with a knife stroke that slices along the inside of the upper jaw. Repeat with the tip of the blade until the mouth is completely and cleanly excavated.

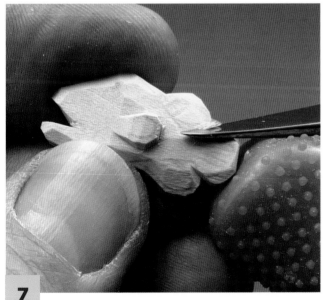

7   **Work on the body.** Draw the centerline of the fish on the top of the figure. Use paring or push cuts to narrow the top of the fish, softening the angle of the edges. Use V-cuts to separate the tail from the top and bottom fins. Working from the side of the fish, first make shallow cuts at the border of the tail and meet those cuts with knife strokes starting at the tips of the fins. Repeat these knife strokes until you reach separation.

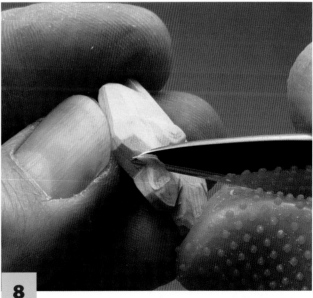

8   **Narrow the fins.** Using stop cuts, narrow both of the fins in front of the tail, top and bottom. Make the first knife strokes on the fins and meet those cuts to chip out the material at the base of fins. Use V-cuts to undercut behind the pectoral fins. Make the first cut on the inside of the fin and meet that cut with a knife stroke slicing flush with the body of the fish. Sand the entire figure smooth with a piece of fine (600–800-grit) sandpaper.

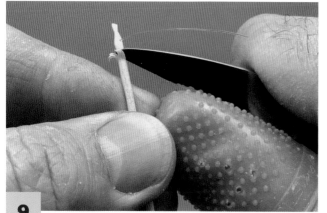

9 **Carve two toothpick fish.** For each fish, roll a toothpick under a sharp blade and snap off the tapered end to form a blunt end. Use paring cuts on opposite sides of the blunt end to form a screwdriver shape. Use V-cuts to form the tail. Make the first knife strokes starting at the tip and meet those cuts with knife strokes in the opposite direction to avoid chipping off the tail. Drill a ⅟₃₂" (0.8mm) hole in the side of the toothpick fish and glue in place a ½" (1.3cm) piece of fishing line using super glue. Use paring cuts to shave around the circumference of the toothpick to form the head and break the fish off from the rest of the toothpick. To aid holding the fish while painting, drill a ⅟₃₂" (0.8mm) hole in the blunted end of a toothpick and super glue the fishing line into the hole. Cut it off when painting is finished.

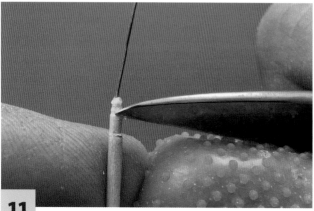

11 **Form the lantern.** Blunt the end of a toothpick by rolling it under a sharp blade and snapping off the taper. Drill a ⅟₃₂" (0.8mm) hole in the blunt end approximately ⅟₁₆" (1.6mm) deep and super glue into place a 1" (2.5cm) piece of 20-gauge bendable wire. When the glue is dry, use paring cuts to taper the blunt end of the toothpick toward the wire. Use shallow V-cuts to build a groove around the circumference of the toothpick at about ⅟₁₆" (1.6mm) from this end. Use V-cuts again to make a bulb about ⅟₁₆" (1.6mm) from the groove, then snap it off. The whole construction should look like a lamp. Cut the wire to ½" (1.3cm) and bend it, drill a ⅟₃₂" (0.8mm) hole in the forehead of the anglerfish, and glue the lantern wire end in place with super glue.

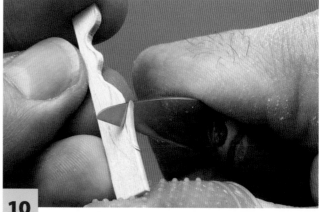

10 **Assemble the box.** Using a miniature table saw or other saw, cut the box pieces to size according to the Materials list. Sand each piece smooth, then glue together all but the sandy seafloor piece in the form of a box (refer to the finished photo if needed). On the sandy seafloor piece, draw a wavy line and use V-cuts to remove all of the material on one side of that line, leaving three sides of the wood straight. Set this piece aside for now (don't attach it). Draw a wavy line at the top quarter of the box and a less wavy line at the bottom third; these demarcate painting areas for later.

12 **Paint each toothpick fish.** Mix small amounts of red, yellow, blue, and white to create a light brown color to paint the entire fish. Use black paint to paint the eyes. Mix black and white for a gray to paint thin lines for the mouth, tail, and pectoral fin. Mix red, blue, yellow, and white to create a reddish brown color to paint the top of the fish and stripes on the side. Use white paint for the reflection in the eye. Add a touch of the brown to white for a cream color to paint lines on the tail and fin.

Pattern

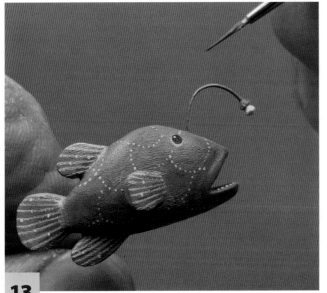
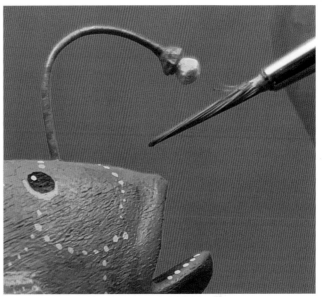

13 **Paint the anglerfish.** Drill a ¹⁄₁₆" (1.6mm) hole in the left side of the anglerfish and insert a toothpick to hold while painting. Mix all five colors to make a muddy gray color; apply this to the fish body, the wire, and the lantern shade. Add more white to the mix and paint the tail and fins. Add white and paint lines on the tail and fins. Add black and water and apply lightly and unevenly over the entire body. Use black paint for the eyes. Add white to the black and paint the inside of the mouth. Mix blue, white, and black; outline the eye and paint random dots on the tail and fins and a trail of dots on the body. Make random white dots on the tail and fins and use white for the reflection in the eye, for the teeth, and for the light. Use yellow to accent the light.

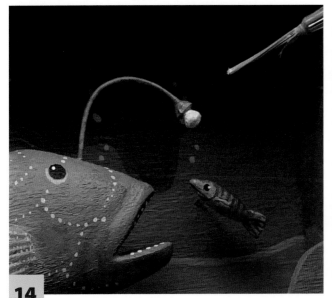

14 **Paint the box.** Paint the outside of the box white. Mix red and yellow to make orange for the sandy seafloor piece. Mix blue, white, red, and yellow for a dark blue to apply to the top inside of the box. Add white to make a light blue for the middle section. Mix all five colors for a brown color to apply to the bottom section. Add white to the brown and outline the boundary between the brown and blue. Mix blue and white to outline the boundary between the two blue sections. Drill a shallow ¹⁄₁₆" (1.6mm) hole on the back face of the box, trim the toothpick holding the anglerfish, and glue in place. Drill ¹⁄₃₂" (0.8mm) holes for the two toothpick fish, trim the fishing line to length, and glue them into place. Finally, glue the sandy seafloor into place.

Cat in a Window

An artist once told me that if you combine cats with hearts in a piece of art, it's guaranteed to sell; using a fake Scottish accent, he called it the "H'arts and Cats movement," a play on words referencing the Arts and Crafts movement of nineteenth century Britain. Cats are popular pets; in photography, a cat perched on a windowsill is a classic image. As if made for each other, the right angles in the window are contrasted and pierced by the playful curves of the cat's tail. Cats are the runway models of the animal world in temperament: they'll sit willingly for hours, then not at all. They are perfect subjects for the portrait artist who should also have photos of the model from all angles to help when painting. I've colored this piece after our own calico cat, but feel free to paint it any other cat color or cover its coat with hearts.

Materials & Tools

- Wood (cat), 1 piece: L-shaped piece with grain running in the direction of the tail; tail section 1" (2.5cm) long, hanging ⅜" (1cm) below the body section; entire piece should be 1³⁄₁₆" (3cm) from head to tail and ¾" (1.9cm) wide; the body section is ⅝" tall x ⅞" long (1.6 x 2.2cm)

  grain running in the longest dimension for all window/box pieces

- Wood (window sill), 1 piece: ⅜" thick x ⅝" wide x 2⁷⁄₁₆" long (1 x 1.6 x 6.2cm)

- Wood (window sides), 2 pieces: ⅜" thick x ⅜" wide x 3¹⁄₁₆" long (1 x 1 x 7.8cm)

- Wood (window top), 1 piece: ⅜" thick x ⅜" wide x 2⁷⁄₁₆" long (1 x 1 x 6.2cm)

- Wood (window vertical crossbar), 1 piece: ³⁄₁₆" thick x ³⁄₁₆" wide x 3¹⁄₁₆" long (4.8mm x 4.8mm x 7.8cm)

- Wood (window horizontal crossbar), 1 piece: ³⁄₁₆" thick x ³⁄₁₆" wide x 1¹¹⁄₁₆" long (4.8mm x 4.8mm x 4.3cm)

- Wood (window back), 1 piece: ¹⁄₁₆" thick x 2" x 3⅜" (1.6mm x 5.1cm x 8.6cm)

- 1 toothpick

- Carving knife

- Hand protection

- Pin vise with ¹⁄₁₆" (1.6mm) drill bit

- Sandpaper: 600–800 grit

- Paintbrushes: #1 or larger round paintbrush, #10/0 liner or smaller detail brush

- Paints: red, blue, yellow, white, and black to mix a variety of colors

- Wood glue

- Miniature table saw (optional) (to cut wood for the box)

Actual size

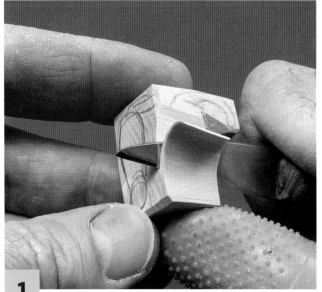

1 **Reduce the wood.** Transfer the cat pattern to the correct piece of wood. Use paring or push cuts to narrow the body section of the wood from ¾" (1.9cm) down to around ⁷⁄₁₆" (1.1cm), leaving a little extra material to remove later.

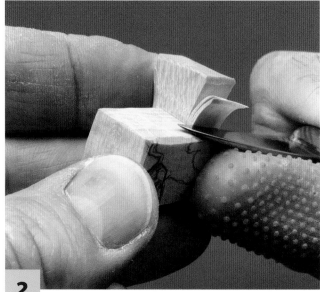

2 **Work near the tail.** Using stop cuts, remove the material from the tail section behind what still remains of the body section. Be careful not to disrupt the flatness of the base of the figure. Make the first knife strokes with the grain, starting at the tip of the tail, directed toward the body. Meet those cuts with knife strokes that slice across the grain, flush with the base of the body.

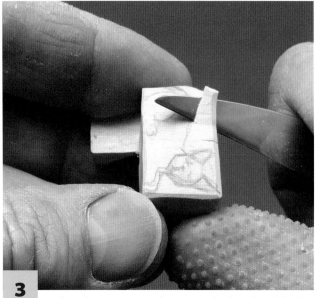

3 **Define the separation between the head and body.** Mark the boundary of the head. Use paring and stop cuts to shorten the height of the body. Start with paring cuts on the side edges at the back end of the figure where the tail connects to the body, then use stop cuts at the transition area between the body and head. Start with knife strokes slicing along the back of the cat and meet those cuts with knife strokes at the boundary with the head.

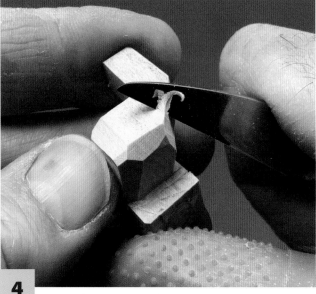

4 **Define the transition from the body to the tail.** Use paring or push cuts to establish the boundary of the tail where it meets the body. Smooth the edges of the tail section and scoop out the material from above the tail where it joins the body. Also remove the bit of material from behind the body on the side opposite from where the tail is dangling so as to define the tail connection point.

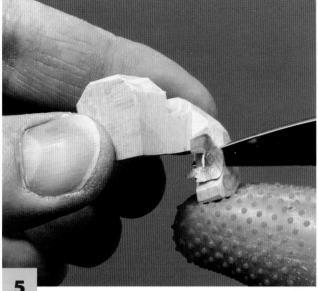

5 **Use V-cuts to shape the curve of the tail.** Start with knife strokes at the tip of the tail and meet those cuts with knife strokes directed down the length of the tail. Use paring and push cuts to smooth the edges of the tail section, leaving extra material to remove later.

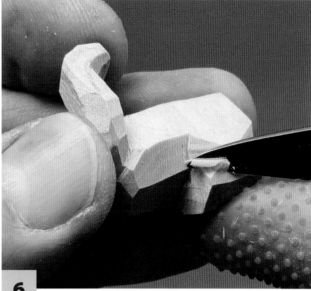

6 **Work on the head.** Use paring or push cuts to remove material from above the head, in front of and behind the ears. Make the knife strokes first at an angle, chopping off the edge and corner of the wood, then use a knife stroke to scoop out the material, and, finally, use a stop cut in front of the ears to square off the junction between the ears and head. On the reverse side, make an angled paring cut from the base to the tip of the ears so that the topmost part is pointy.

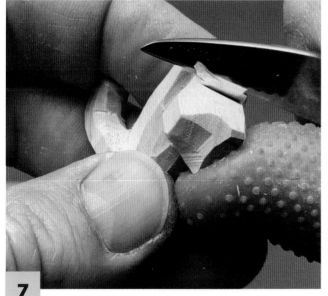

7 **Create a border at the bottom of the head.** Use V-cuts under the chin. Make the first knife strokes from the chin and meet those cuts from the top of the front legs. Use V-cuts on the right side of the head above the paws to create separation between the paws and head, make the first strokes at the top of the paws at an angle toward the head, and meet those cuts with knife strokes from the side of the head.

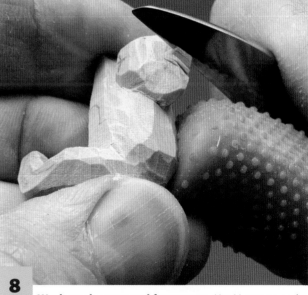

8 **Work on the ears and front paws.** Use V-cuts to make a notch between the ears to separate them. Continue making V-cuts until the notch reaches the top of the head. Use V-cuts to make a notch between the left and right paws to separate them. Use just the tip of the blade so as not to cut into the side of the head.

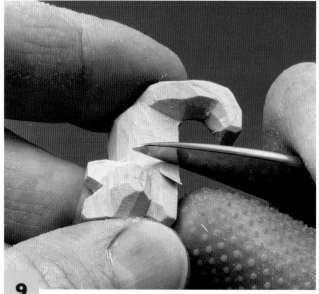

9 **Establish the back legs.** First, use stop cuts to establish the forward-most reach of the rear paws. Start with a knife stroke in front of the paw directed toward the tail and meet that cut with a knife stroke at the border of the paw that chops off the chip. Next, make combination cuts above the paws. Start with a knife stroke flush with the top of the paw directed toward the tail and meet the end of that cut with a knife stroke from above. The third knife stroke that meets the previous two in the recess between the paw and leg will chip out the chunk of material there, leaving a notch that defines the rear leg.

10 **Refine the ears.** Use paring or push cuts to widen the notch between the ears. Make knife strokes starting at the base of each ear, directed toward the tip of each ear. Narrow the depth of each ear in a similar fashion. Compare the ears to each other and remove excess material from whichever is larger.

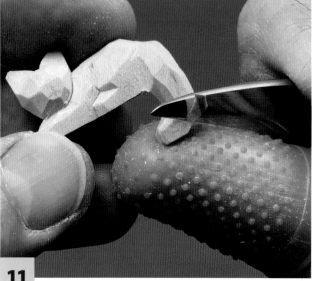

11 **Refine the tail.** Use paring and push cuts to make the finishing touches to the tail. Smooth the angled edges and make certain the curves look natural and playful. Use V-cuts on the inside of the curves, always starting the first knife strokes at the tip and meeting those cuts with knife strokes from the opposite direction.

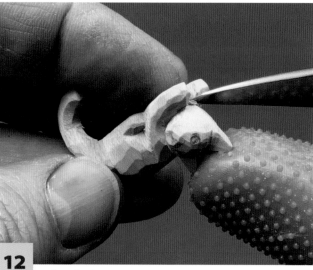

12 **Refine the front paws and face.** Make combination cuts between the front paws and legs. Expand the gap between the front paws with a three-stroke cut. Make the first two cuts on the inside edges of the paws and connect those cuts with a third from underneath. Continue this combination of cuts until the gap reaches the slope of the neck. Finally, use paring and push cuts to refine the face, making the muzzle area thinner than the forehead and rounding the edges of the head. Finally, drill a 1/16" (1.6mm) hole in the bottom of the figure and insert a toothpick to hold while painting.

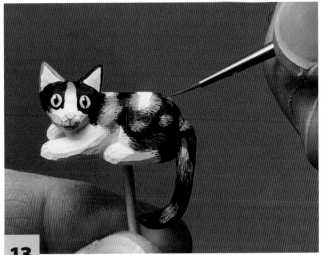

13 **Paint the cat.** Mix white, yellow, and red to create a cream color for the base. Mix white, yellow, and blue for light green for the eyes. Use black for the pupils and the pattern on the rest of the cat. Mix all five colors to make a rusty brown shade for the brown pattern. Use black to make lines protruding into the brown and make white lines protruding into the black. Paint the white eye reflection. Mix black, white, and yellow for gray to paint the mouth and outline under the nose. Mix white, yellow, and red to make pink; paint the inside of the ears and the nose.

14 **Assemble and paint the window.** Using a saw, cut the box pieces to size according to the Materials list and sand each piece smooth. Make squared notches at the midpoints of the two crossbar pieces and fit them together like a cross. Glue all but the back together. Paint the entire frame white. Mix white and blue; paint the back piece. Pencil in branched lines. Create a range of pink hues mixing white, red, and yellow and paint clusters of cherry blossoms along the branches. Apply the hues randomly to the blossoms. Use black to paint branches, including inside the blossom clusters. Mix black, white, and yellow for a gray to outline one side of the branch. Glue the back piece to the frame and glue the cat in place. Drill a ¹⁄₁₆" (1.6mm) hole on the back of the frame for hanging.

Patterns

African Safari

The word "safari" comes from the Swahili language, meaning journey; in the West, it's come to mean the quintessential adventure, a trip into the heart of Africa to see animals in their natural habitat and to take pictures of them. The experience has taken on a culture of its own, complete with Range Rovers, pith helmets, and khaki clothing. I've never been on safari, but I've tried to recreate the spectacle with staged woodcarvings in a manner that could best be described as nature photography for the control freak. In this tableau, the weather is always perfect and the animal smiles for the camera; there's no danger of lions attacking, and, even if they did, at less than 1" (2.5cm) long, their bites would be no more painful than that of a gnat. This particular safari takes place in the shadow of Mount Kilimanjaro and features a giraffe. The tiny middle ground tree helps blend the foreground with the background.

The wide frame around this project is an optional add-on not reflected in the Materials & Tools list or instructions.

Materials & Tools

grain running in the longest dimension for all pieces

- Wood (giraffe), 1 piece: ⅜" x ¼" x 1" (1 x 6.4mm x 2.5cm)
- Wood (large tree), 1 piece: ¼" thick x ¾" wide x 1⅛" tall (6.4mm x 1.9cm x 2.9cm)
- Wood (small tree), 1 piece: ⅛" thick x ⅜" wide x ½" tall (3.2mm x 1cm x 1.3cm)
- Wood (tree line), 1 piece: ³⁄₃₂" thick x ⅜" wide x 3¼" long (2.4mm x 1cm x 8.3cm)
- Wood (box back), 1 piece: ³⁄₆₄" thick x 2³⁄₃₂" x 3⁹⁄₁₆" (1.2mm x 5.3cm x 9cm)
- Wood (box top and bottom): 2 pieces: ⁵⁄₃₂" thick x 2³⁄₃₂" wide x 3⁹⁄₁₆" long (4mm x 1.8cm x 9cm)
- Wood (box sides), 2 pieces: ⁵⁄₃₂" thick x 2³⁄₃₂" wide x 2¼" long (4mm x 1.8cm x 5.7cm)

- Several toothpicks
- Carving knife
- Detail knife
- Hand protection
- Pin vise with ¹⁄₁₆" (1.6mm) and ¹⁄₃₂" (0.8mm) drill bits
- Sandpaper: 600–800 grit
- Paintbrushes: #1 or larger round paintbrush, #10/0 liner or smaller detail brush
- Paints: red, blue, yellow, white, and black to mix a variety of colors
- Wood glue
- Miniature table saw (optional) (to cut wood for the box)
- Tweezers (optional)

Actual size
(excluding optional frame)

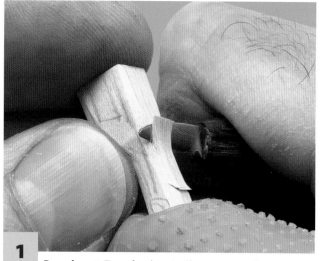

1 **Rough out.** Transfer the giraffe pattern to the correct piece of wood. Use paring or push cuts to remove the wood from behind the head and neck, leaving the material for the ears untouched. Use V-cuts under the head and in front of the neck to remove the material there. Start with knife strokes at the chin and meet those cuts with strokes from in front of the lower neck. Use paring or push cuts to narrow the entire head and neck region to around ⅛" (3.2mm).

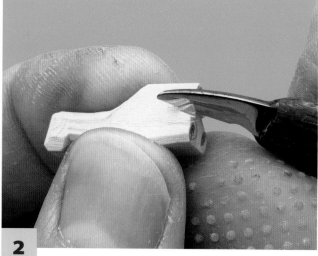

2 **Work the legs.** Draw the hoofprints on the bottom of the piece of wood in the four corners. Use V-cuts to separate the front from back and left from right legs. Start with knife strokes on the sides of the figure on the bottom between the legs. Make matched cuts on all four sides to produce V-shaped notches. Make two V-cuts on the bottom of the figure in the form of a cross between the legs, connecting the newly carved notches.

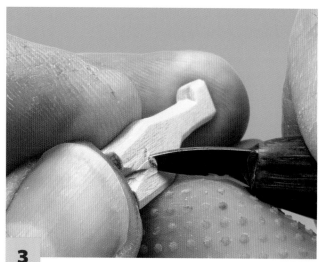

3 **Continue work on the legs.** Make three-stroke combination cuts at the location of the notches between the legs. Make the first two knife strokes parallel to the legs, slicing toward the belly. Angle the cuts toward each other so that they meet at a point near the midpoint of the belly. Make a third knife stroke flush with the belly, connecting the two previous cuts and chipping out the wood between them. Make a series of slicing strokes between the legs, first parallel to the legs, then angled from one side to the other so as to chip out the wood. Finish with a jabbing knife stroke at the base of the legs to chip out the remaining material.

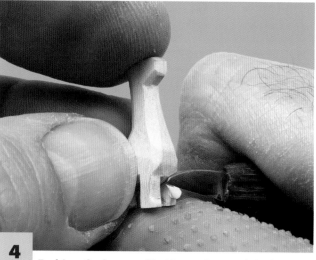

4 **Fashion the hooves.** Use V-cuts. Start with knife strokes from the tip of each hoof and meet that cut with knife strokes from the front of the leg. It's important that you proceed in that order, or you risk losing the hoof. With these secondary knife strokes, narrow the legs and, on the rear legs, start to establish the bend in the leg. Use paring or push cuts to narrow the nose and round the edges of the head in front of the horns.

5

Define the ears and horns. Use V-cuts to establish the boundaries of the ears and horns. For the ears, start with knife strokes from the tip of the ears, slicing toward the back of the neck and chopping out the material with knife strokes from the back of the neck. Do the same for the top of the ear: start at the tip and slice toward the back of the head, chipping out this material with knife strokes that meet the first cuts, starting at the back of the horns. For the horns, make knife strokes at the forehead, toward the horns, and meet the cuts with strokes beginning at the front tip of the horn, directed downward toward the head. On the backside of the horns, start with knife strokes at the back of the head directed toward the horns, and meet those cuts with knife strokes directed down the back of the horns. All of these cuts are extremely tiny and need to be precisely executed or you'll lose the horns and ears.

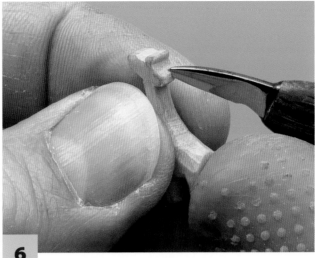

6

Separate the left and right ears and horns. Use V-cuts at the midpoint of both the ears and horns to create a notch that separates the left from the right. Square off the V-shaped notches with stop cuts by slicing along the insides of the base of each ear or horn, flush with the top of the head, then meet those cuts with knife strokes on the insides of the features. Narrow the ears and horns from the outside with stop cuts. Make the first cut flush with the head at the base of the horn or ear and meet that cut with a knife stroke from the tip to the base of the feature.

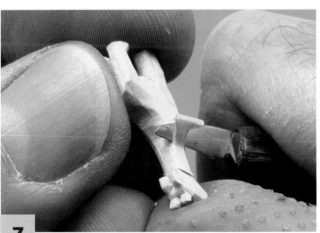

7

Finish and sand the body. Use stop cuts to narrow the neck and establish the cheeks. Start with knife strokes at the cheeks, directed at an angle toward the neck. Meet those cuts with knife strokes from the neck. Use a V-cut to make a small V-shaped notch for the mouth. Sand the entire figure with 600–800-grit sandpaper. Use the sandpaper not only to smooth the surface, but also to add more definition to the smallest features. Be careful not to over-sand or create ridges. Where needed, use a detail knife to remove material and refine features.

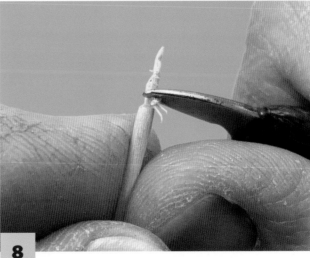

8

Make the tail. Use paring cuts to whittle the pointed end of a toothpick to a slightly curved tail section ³⁄₃₂" (2.4mm) long. Use paring cuts to establish the beginning of the brushy part of the tail and shave around the circumference of the toothpick another ³⁄₃₂" (2.4mm) further to separate the tail from the rest of the toothpick. Make a shallow vertical notch in the rear end of the giraffe and use wood glue to attach the tail to the body. A pair of tweezers is helpful for this. Finally, drill a ¹⁄₃₂" (1mm) hole in the bottom of the figure and glue in place a toothpick to hold while painting.

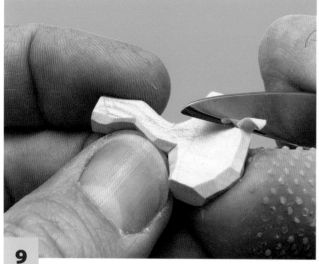

9 **Start the large tree.** Transfer the large tree pattern onto the correct piece of wood. Use paring or push cuts to remove the material on both sides of the trunk. Where the trunk meets the foliage, use stop cuts to establish the boundary. Start with knife strokes along the bottom of the foliage region and meet those cuts with knife strokes from the trunk. Leave a wider bit of material near the area of transition for the branches. Use V-cuts to separate the foliage area into around a dozen distinct chunks of various shapes and sizes.

10 **Finish the large tree.** Use stop cuts to narrow the area where the trunk meets the foliage. Start with knife strokes at the base of the foliage and meet those cuts with knife strokes from the trunk. Use paring cuts to fashion the outside boundaries of the branching region. Draw the branches, then use three-stroke combination cuts between the front and back branches to establish gaps between them. Start with a pair of knife strokes from the crook of each branch, slicing flush with the branch and directed toward the foliage region. Make the third knife stroke flush with the underside of the foliage to chip out a triangular piece of wood. Repeat these knife strokes until there is a clean separation between the branches. Then make a smaller tree using these same, albeit simplified instructions, from the correct piece of wood.

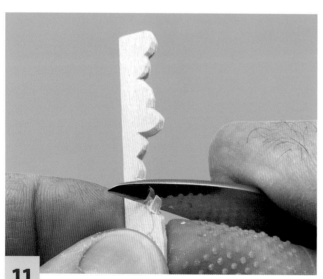

11 **Assemble the box.** Using a miniature table saw or other saw, cut the box pieces to size according to the Materials list. Sand each piece smooth, then glue together all but the tree line piece in the form of a box (refer to the finished photo if needed). For the tree line, cut the piece out, then draw a random pattern of small undulating, rounded bumps along the length of the wood and use V-cuts to remove the material above the line. Use paring cuts to create a bevel on the front side of each bump. Set this piece aside for now (don't attach it).

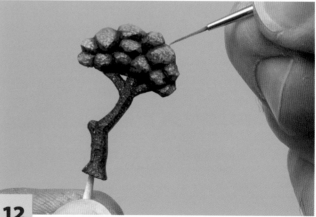

12 **Paint the trees.** Drill 1/16" (1.6mm) holes in the bottoms of the trees and insert toothpicks to hold while painting. Mix blue and yellow to create a green color, then paint the foliage. Add black to part of the green mixture and paint in the crevices between the lumps of foliage. Add yellow to the other part of the green mixture and paint random spots on the foliage lumps. Give the trunk a base coat of black. Mix red, yellow, and blue to make brown, then paint random hash marks on the trunk. Add more yellow to the brown and paint small dots on the trunk. Paint the smaller tree in a similar fashion.

13 **Paint the giraffe.** Mix yellow, white, and red to create a light yellow to paint a base coat. Add white and paint the inside of the ears. Mix black, white, and yellow to make a gray color, then paint the hooves. Paint the eyes black. Add white reflective dots in each eye. Mix red, yellow, blue, and white to create a brown color, and paint a dot pattern over the entire body. Add yellow to the brown mixture and paint dots on the legs.

14 **Start painting the background.** Draw the shape of the mountain. Mix blue and white to create a light blue to paint the sky. Mix blue, red, and white to make purple to paint the mountain. Mix a watery yellow to apply to the sky on both sides of the mountain and blend. Use white to paint the snowcap. Add blue to the white and paint the left half of the snowcap. Mix blue, red, and white to create a bluer version of the purple you used for the mountain, and make streaks on the mountainside. Mix yellow with the purple to create a brown color; add water and apply lightly to the lower half of the mountain.

15 **Finish painting.** Mix yellow, white, and red to make gold to paint the grass. Mix blue, yellow, and white for a green color to use as a base for the tree line piece. Add white to the mix and paint highlights to each foliage lump. Mix red, yellow, and blue to create a brown for the lower edge of the tree line and highlight the border with the foliage with yellow. Apply a wash of yellow to the grass field. Glue in place the tree line, the two trees, and the giraffe with wood glue. Mix red, yellow, and blue to create a brown to apply scribbles to the grass field. Add white to the brown and make more scribbles and hash marks.

Patterns

Moby Dick

The oceans are still as yet not fully explored; they are the frontier on our doorstep, and they're as alien as the reaches of outer space. Scientists predict that we've identified only a small fraction of the creatures living within, and the whale is, by size, the king of this deep unknown. There's something oddly compelling about seeing a scene of massive energy and destruction safely in the confines of a box that could fit in a shirt pocket. This piece, based on the story of Moby Dick, is a relic of history, when street lamps burned whale fat and sailors tended actual sails. Those sails used here are literally wood chips, sliced and cut to shape in a manner I find particularly pleasing, since one is using what is usually considered the waste product to represent the sole means of oceanic locomotion for this age.

The wide frame around this project is an optional add-on not reflected in the Materials & Tools list or instructions.

Materials & Tools

grain running in the longest dimension for all pieces

- Wood (whale), 1 piece: ⅜" x ⅜" x 1" (1 x 1 x 2.5cm)
- Wood (ship), 1 piece: ⅛" thick x ⁵⁄₃₂" wide x ½" long (3.2mm x 4mm x 1.3cm)
- Wood (sails), 1 piece: ⅛" (3.2mm)
- Wood (box back), 1 piece: ¹⁄₁₆" thick x 2¹⁄₁₆" wide x 3¹⁄₁₆" long (1.6mm x 5.2cm x 7.8cm)
- Wood (box top and bottom), 2 pieces: ³⁄₁₆" thick x ²²⁄₃₂" wide x 1 ¹¹⁄₁₆" long (4.8mm x 1.7cm x 4.3cm)
- Wood (box sides), 2 pieces: ³⁄₁₆" thick x ²²⁄₃₂" wide x 3¹⁄₁₆" long (4.8mm x 1.7cm x 7.8cm)

- Several toothpicks
- Carving knife
- Hand protection
- Pin vise with ¹⁄₁₆" (1.6mm) and ¹⁄₃₂" (0.8mm) drill bits
- Sandpaper: 600–800 grit
- Paintbrushes: #1 or larger round paintbrush, #10/0 liner or smaller detail brush
- Paints: red, blue, yellow, white, and black to mix a variety of colors
- Wood glue
- Miniature table saw (optional) (to cut wood for the box)
- Tweezers (optional)

Actual size
(excluding optional frame)

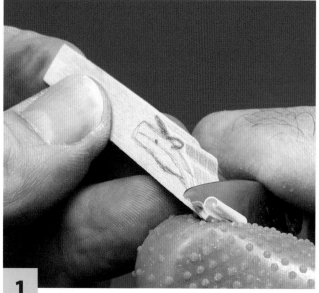

1 **Rough out the whale.** Transfer the whale pattern to the correct piece of wood. Use paring or push cuts to remove material from below the belly and tail. Leave material for the pectoral fins, and leave the tail area approximately 1/16" (1.6mm) thick for strength while you carve the rest of the figure.

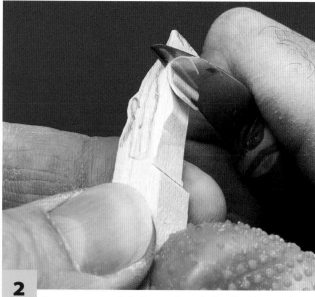

2 **Remove material above the whale.** Use V-cuts above the head and body to remove material in front of the tail. Make the first knife strokes at the base of the tail, directed toward the head. Meet those cuts with knife strokes from the head, directed toward the tail. Leave some material for the dorsal fins.

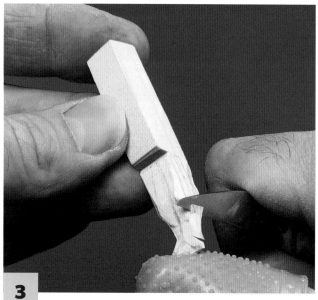

3 **Narrow the body in front of the tail.** Use V-cuts to narrow the transition from the tail to the body. Start with knife strokes around 1/16" (1.6mm) in front of the outermost tips of the tail directed at an angle toward the head so as to leave approximately 1/16" (1.6mm) of additional material in front of the tail section on both sides. Meet these cuts with knife strokes from the middle of the body directed toward the tail.

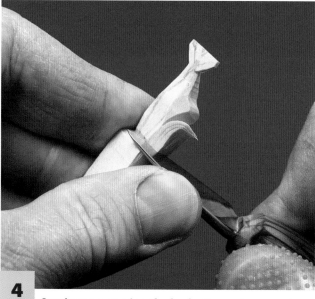

4 **Continue narrowing the body.** Use paring or push cuts to narrow the sides of the body and head in front of the pectoral fins. Start the knife strokes at the tips of the fins directed toward the head. Angle the cuts so that the fin section tapers in toward the body.

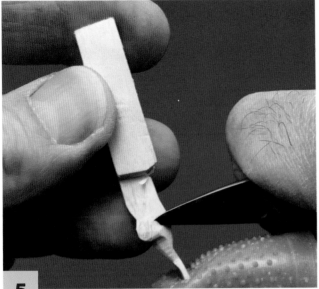

5 **Define the pectoral fins.** Use stop cuts on the top of the pectoral fins to remove the material there. Start with a knife stroke at the top edge of the fin to establish its boundary and meet that cut with a knife stroke running flush with the body that chips out the wood. Be careful not to cut too deep to avoid damaging the fin.

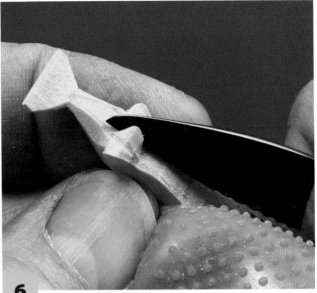

6 **Separate the left and right pectoral fins.** On the underside of the figure, use stop cuts to define the left and right pectoral fins. First, make shallow cuts parallel to and about 1/16" (1.6mm) from the outside plane of the fin. Meet those cuts with knife strokes from the midpoint of the figure. Remove the material between the fins with a knife stroke that runs flush with the belly.

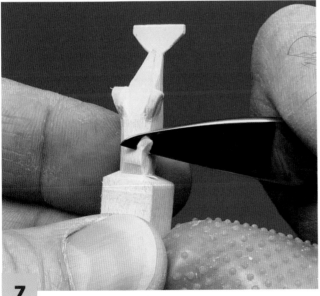

7 **Work on the head.** Use paring cuts, then stop cuts to define the mouth. Make the paring cuts at the bottom edge of the head, then use paring cuts. With the first knife strokes, establish the border on both sides of the lower jaw, then meet those cuts with shallow knife strokes that scoop from the base of the jaw. Make sure that the blade tip only reaches the cut and does not slice deeper.

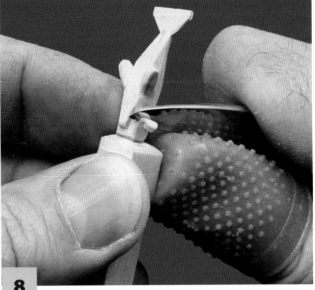

8 **Finish the whale.** Use paring cuts to smooth the edges and refine the whale to its final dimensions. Narrow the fins slightly from the outside and the tail from the bottom. Use controlled knife strokes that only remove small amounts of material. Next, use fine (600–800-grit) sandpaper to further shape and refine the figure, paying special attention to the edges of the fins and tail and the gap between the lower jaw and the head. Release the whale from its holding block and sand the nose.

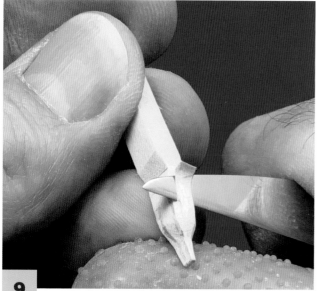

9 **Rough out the ship.** Transfer the ship hull pattern to the correct piece of wood. Use paring or push cuts to narrow the sides, round the front and bottom, and establish the bowsprit (the long pole protruding from the front of the sailing ship).

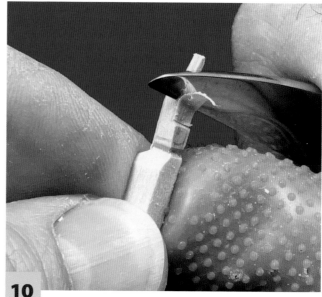

10 **Make the ship's decks.** Use a stop cut to establish the two levels of the deck of the ship. Use the first knife stroke to establish the border between the two levels and meet that cut with knife strokes that start at the base of the bowsprit and slice toward the back of the ship. Make knife strokes on both sides at the back of the ship to slice it off from the piece of wood.

11 **Finish the ship.** Sand the hull of the ship with fine (600–800-grit) sandpaper. Drill one ¹⁄₁₆" (1.6mm) hole in the bottom of the ship to insert a toothpick for holding. Drill four holes on the top, along the centerline of the deck, each ¹⁄₃₂" (0.8mm) in diameter. Whittle down and sand four pieces of toothpick to fit the four holes to act as masts. Make the two inside masts ³⁄₈" (1cm) tall and the front and rear masts ³⁄₁₆" (4.8mm) tall. Use a piece of wood approximately ⅛" (3.2mm) wide to carve several long wood chips. Cut the chips for sails, two each rectangular sails for the middle masts, a triangular sail for the front mast, and a four-sided trapezoidal shape for the rear mast. Apply glue to the masts with a toothpick and use tweezers to pick up and attach the sails to their respective masts.

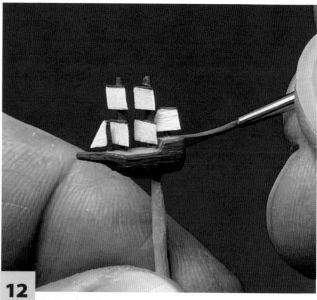

12 **Paint the ship.** Mix blue, red, and yellow to create a brown color to paint the entire ship except for the deck and sails. Add yellow to the brown for a lighter brown and paint the deck. Mix white with the light brown to make a cream color and paint the sails. Mix the rest of the brown with black and paint thin lines along the sides of the ship.

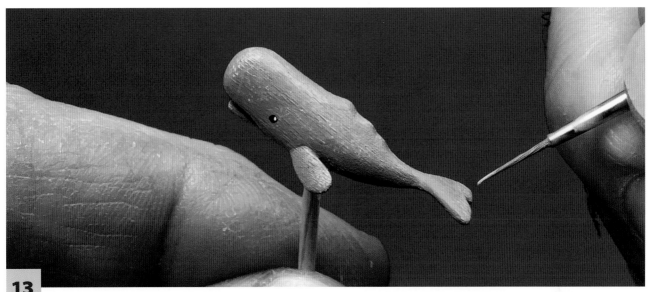

13   **Paint the whale.** Drill a ¹⁄₁₆" (1.6mm) hole in the bottom of the figure and insert a toothpick to hold while painting. Mix black, white, and a touch of yellow to make gray for the base coat. Use black for the eyes. Paint the white reflection dots. Mix white into the gray and use it to make small dots and scratches on the whale, focusing on the tips of the fins and tail, the area around the mouth, and the front of the head.

14   **Assemble and paint the box.** Using a saw, cut the box pieces to size according to the Materials list. Sand smooth, then glue together all the pieces. Paint the outside black. Draw a wavy line and a curvy line inside the box, dividing it in thirds. Using blue, black, and white, create three gradations of blue and apply them to the three regions. Mix blue and white for a light blue and outline the wavy line. Add blue for a darker light blue and outline the rolling line. Drill a ¹⁄₃₂" (1mm) hole in the whale and glue and peg the ship to the whale. Drill a hole in the back of the box; glue and peg the whale to the box. Mix blue and white for a light blue and paint dots around the whale.

Patterns

Resources

Of all the resources at our disposal, the Internet offers a bounty for all aspects of a woodcarver's needs, albeit with some caveats. For ideas and painting schemes, a simple search reveals an abundance of options, but beware of the tendency in online photography toward oversaturated color and color shift. Additionally, many of the social network apps have virtual carving clubs, but without a physical presence, they are a far cry from sitting around a warm oven with a cup of joe and a tribe of witty whittlers. Still, they are friendly spaces to get advice and support. Likewise, projects, classes, and basic information are on offer for free on YouTube and, for a fee and with more individual attention, on platforms like Zoom. Finally, wood and tools are easy to find in online stores. Take what you can from what is offered there from the comfort of your home and seek out authentic experience when you are able.

Back in the real world, local carving clubs offer a way to grow friendships, meet teachers, and learn new skills. If your region doesn't have a club, consider starting something by finding a couple interested people through message boards online, in senior centers, libraries, grocery stores, or wherever your community meets. Attending arts and crafts fairs, open studio events, and woodcarving exhibitions can put you in touch with people who may have the knowledge and connections you are looking for, whether it's tools, material, techniques, creative spaces, or sales opportunities. Folk schools that teach traditional crafts often offer classes from reputable carvers that focus on specific projects, and some carvers offer basic classes for beginners.

Finally, get out to walk in nature if and when you can; it's a free resource for both inspiration and regeneration. Plus, after sitting for hours, it's a benefit both mentally and physically. A slow walk in the woods, without purpose or intent, can bring a sense of awareness and well-being that cannot be duplicated through any other experience. If weather and bugs permit, bring your carving kit and use that time to get away from it all and whittle away the hours.

About the Author

Steve Tomashek grew up in Winona, Minnesota, the youngest of seven kids in a household steeped in arts and crafts, including woodcarving. He is a graduate of Indiana University, where he studied World History and earned a teaching certificate. Encouraged by a coworker and guided by a course titled "Self Instruction in Art," he took up whittling as a way of making peace with a fire that destroyed his family's house, including a workshop full of his grandpa's tools. After college and several years of practice, he quit a teaching job to pursue carving as a full time career.

For twenty-five years, Steve has worked through galleries, gift shops, and at art fairs, selling his carvings in both the U.S. and Germany. It was during his first trip to Germany in 2009 to see a Christmas market or "Weihnachtsmarkt" that he met his future wife. He moved there two years later and they got married. Since then, he's also become a father and a farmer. Now with a talkative toddler and a barnyard of animals to care for, the changes have informed his work and moved his skills and interests toward convergence in the form of children's stories featuring his own writing and illustrations.

Index